*This book is lovingly dedicated
to my wife, Donna,
whose many hours of editing
and helpful suggestions
made it all possible.
The world is a better place,
and this is a better book
because of her!*

Contents

1

Who Does God Want to Heal?

My evangelistic ministry has taken me to the four corners of the globe where thousands have been healed through the prayer of faith. I am frequently approached by some desperate person who asks, "Why wasn't *I* healed?" All around him he sees the deaf responding to sound after years of silence, crutches being discarded, paralytics literally leaping for joy, and he says, "I've been prayed for and I'm still sick. How come?"

The question haunted me. It deserved a reply. But my search for any easy answer failed. No one solution, no magic formula applies to all situations. But surely with a God who said, "Come now and let us reason together..." (Isaiah 1:18a KJV), there had to be some answers somewhere. But where?

9

Where else, but in God's Word? And the deeper I probed the Scriptures, the more truth I unearthed. This book is the result of those months of prayerful research. There are many books dealing with the scriptural validity of divine healing, and it is not my intention to add to those. My sole intent in writing this book is to help that person who already believes in his right to divine healing, but who has not yet received the promised healing. My sincere desire is that as he reads this, new hope, new courage, new faith will come to him to believe for a miracle! So read this book prayerfully, with a totally open and sincere heart, listening carefully for the voice of the Holy Spirit as He might speak to *you.*

I have heard ministers and well-meaning Christians say to a desperate person who had not received healing: "Take it! Receive it! It's yours! There's *no reason* why you can't have it!"

But this isn't necessarily so. There are indeed reasons why some people aren't healed. But it *is* God's will to heal every born-again believer, when the conditions are met.

One of the greatest controversies in the Christian Church today is whether or not God heals and, if He does, does He want to heal everyone? Well, what does the Bible say about this subject? It is imperative that we have a knowledge of the Word and will of God in order that the prayer of faith can be offered.

In the book of Hebrews, it is written of Christ: "Then I said, just as I was commanded in the scroll of the book, 'God here I am! Coming to obey your will' " (Hebrews 10:7 Phillips).

Christ Himself said, "For I have come here from heaven to do the will of God who sent me, not to have my own way" (John 6:38 TLB). And ". . . My food is to do the

10

will of Him who sent me . . ." (John 4:34 JB). We may logically conclude that everything Jesus did was in direct fulfillment of the will of God.

A leper came to Jesus seeking healing. As an outcast of society, he was unable to mingle with healthy people. Thus he probably was not familiar with all that Christ was doing in His healing ministry. He approached the Master with the statement, " 'If you want to, you can make me clean.' Jesus, filled with pity for him, stretched out his hand and placed it on the leper saying, 'Of course I want to—be clean' " (Mark 1:40 Phillips). These Scriptures show it *is* God's will to heal all who come to Him in faith.

I like the way Jesus answered the leper, "*Of course* I want to," as though there were no question concerning His willingness to do so. His reply is so strongly *affirmative* that it leaves no room for doubt as to His will.

Now let's consider Jesus' actions. Since His actions would have to be in direct alignment with the will of God (He said He did *nothing* but what the Father showed Him), by reading what He did, we will have a revelation of the will of God.

". . . Large crowds followed him, and he healed them all" (Matthew 12:15b Phillips).

"And all who were ill were brought to him, and he was begged to allow them simply to touch the edge of his cloak. And everyone who touched it was completely cured!" (Matthew 14:35b-36 NEB).

"And everyone in the crowd was trying to touch him because power came out of him that cured them all" (Luke 6:19 JB).

"You must have heard how God anointed him with the power of the Holy Spirit, of how he went about doing good, and healing all who suffered

11

under the devil's power— because God was with him" (Acts 10:38 Phillips).

"As the sun went down that evening, all the villagers who had any sick people in their homes, no matter what their diseases were, brought them to Jesus; and the touch of His hands healed every one" (Luke 4:40 TLB).

Jesus *never* refused to heal anyone who came to Him in faith. One day a Syrophoenician woman (a pagan Gentile) came to Jesus begging Him to cast a demon out of her daughter. It seems as though the Lord refused to help her at first. But let's consider the story more closely.

Jesus had come to the Jews, knowing that they would reject Him and that the Gentiles would be given a chance to receive eternal life later. Up until this point all the blessings that flowed from Christ were aimed at the Jews, and this woman had no right to any of these privileges yet. So He answered her, "You must let the children have all they want first. It is not right, you know, to take the children's food and throw it to the dogs" (Mark 7:27 Phillips).

The Gentiles would have their fill, but not just yet. Jesus was not refusing, but rather deferring. However, He did an abrupt reversal and cast the demon out of the girl. The beauty of this story is that the desire of the Lord is always to honor faith wherever He finds it, even if it means altering His own plans to do so!

The prophet Isaiah wrote of Christ the Messiah saying, "Surely he hath borne our griefs [diseases]—and carried our sorrows [pains]..." (Isaiah 53:4 KJV). Some argue that Isaiah's reference to griefs (*diseases* in the original Hebrew and translated that way in every other reference) and sorrows (literally *pains* in Hebrew) are meant to

12

convey spiritual overtones, and do not refer to physical healing. Matthew 8:16 alludes to that very prophecy, "That evening they brought unto him many who were possessed by devils. He cast out the spirits with a word, and cured all who were sick. This was to fulfill the prophecy of Isaiah: 'He took our sicknesses away and carried our diseases for us' " (JB).

So He has borne our sicknesses as well as our sins, and just as effectively. No Christian would doubt for a moment that the penalty of all our sins was paid on Calvary, for He bore them in our place. Yet many of these same people doubt divine healing, carrying their own sicknesses, even though He has borne them already.

"Who forgiveth all thine iniquities; who healeth all thy diseases" (Psalm 103:3 KJV). God has always intended that the forgiveness of sins and the healing of the physical body should go hand in hand. Notice in the New Testament how often the Lord healed and forgave individuals at the same moment.

An Old Testament example of this can be found in the book of Numbers. The Israelites had begun to murmur against God, complaining about everything. As a consequence, God sent fiery serpents among them and many who were bitten died.

"And the Lord said unto Moses, 'Make thee a fiery serpent, and set it upon a pole: and it shall come to pass, that every one that is bitten, when he looketh upon it, shall live, . . . And it came to pass, that if a serpent had bitten any man, when he beheld the serpent of brass, he lived" (Numbers 21:8, 9b KJV). God healed everyone who did as He had commanded. All who looked were forgiven—all who looked were healed!

I suppose the greatest display of God's healing occurred

in Egypt when God was preparing to bring the Israelites out of their four hundred years of bondage. They had been physically as well as mentally and spiritually abused for centuries. Their work load had been severely increased and the equipment to do the work had been taken away. At the same time, their food rations had been cut, so that vast numbers were sick and on the verge of death. Yet we are told, "He [God] brought them forth . . . and there was not one feeble person among their tribes" (Psalm 105:37 KJV). What a fantastic scene that must have been as the power of God swept over two to three million people, and *healed every one of them!*

When God wanted to reveal Himself (His nature) to the children of Israel, He told them: ". . . I am the Lord that healeth thee" (Exodus 15:26 KJV). He was then and still is today the God who heals the sick and afflicted. God never changes. What He was a million years ago, He is today and will be a million years from now. God never becomes less to His children in succeeding generations. And He reveals more and more of Himself as each dispensation unfolds.

Jesus continued to do what the Father had done in the Old Testament. He healed the sick everywhere He went. The Father had been *Jehovah Raphah,* "the Lord that healeth thee." Jesus said, "Anyone who has seen me has seen the Father. Then how can you say, 'Show us the Father?' Do you not believe that I am in the Father, and the Father in me? I am not myself the source of the words I speak to you: it is the Father who dwells in me doing His own work" (John 14:9b, 10 NEB). So here we have a clear-cut revelation that God was *continuing* His work in the person of Christ.

We find further substantiation in Malachi 3:6 (KJV),

"For I am the Lord, I change not"; and in Hebrews 13:8 (JB), "Jesus Christ is the same today as he was yesterday and as he will be forever." In Malachi, ending the Old Testament, God showed Himself as One who never changes. In the New Testament, in the person of Christ, He continued to do His works. The book of Hebrews tells us that He will continue to be whatever He has been in ages past. We, the Church, are His body and He continues His work and demonstrates His graces through us as the Father did through the Son. *He never changes!*

It is strange that so many believers read the Scriptures and doubt that God still heals miraculously. If these truths were taken into a court as evidence and given a fair trial by jury, no one could reach any other conclusion than that divine healing *is* for today, and that it is for every believer. The facts stand for themselves. No one can alter them.

Ask the many thousands who have been healed as I have prayed the prayer of faith for them—the blind who now see, the crippled who now walk, the deaf who now hear, those with cancer or tumors who are now healthy, those with twisted, deformed limbs who now stand straight and whole—ask them! They stand as testimony that the Word of God works, and that God will heal those who have faith in His Word. What He has done for others, He will do for you. "The truth I have now come to realize, he said, is that God does not have favorites" (Acts 10:34 JB).

2

Why Doesn't God Heal Everyone?

If God wants to heal everyone, then why doesn't He? That's a valid question. If God *does* want to heal everyone, why isn't everyone robust and well; why is there so much ill health in the world today?

God abides in the domain of the miraculous, and man abides there only when he walks in strict obedience to the revealed will of the Father. It is only proper and just for God to place upon man certain conditions that govern his access to the supernatural. When only a little was known of the nature of God, He required little of man.

We must understand that those who lived in Bible times were not privileged to freely handle the Word of God as we do. In fact, the average man was forbidden by the religious leaders to touch the scrolls, lest he defile them. Until a few hundred years ago there was no version of the Scriptures in the language of the common man. And even when it became available, most people were too poor to own a Bible.

In the course of time, as God's mysteries unfolded (through His Word), we became responsible for these truths and precepts. Where once He healed almost indiscriminately, He now requires more of His creation. Jesus said, "Much is required from those to whom much is given, for their responsibility is greater" (Luke 12:48b TLB).

We are a fortunate people—not only can we purchase a Bible at will, but now we have many fine translations in contemporary language.

Of course, with every privilege comes responsibility. We must learn the demands of God now placed upon us so that we may be healed.

God has not changed. He still longs to cure all who will trust Him as their Healer, but He has certain conditions which must be met before the laws of divine health become operable. These conditions are as certain as any of the known laws of physics—the rising of the sun in the east, the earth's rotation at given speeds, and the changing of the seasons. True, God has sometimes suspended these laws or brought into play some higher law of physics unknown to man. Didn't He stop the sun in its course for Joshua? "Sun, stand thou still upon Gibeon; and thou, moon in the valley of Ajalon" (Joshua 10:12b KJV).

And didn't He set the sundial back ten degrees at the prophet Isaiah's request? "Behold, I will bring again the shadow of the degrees, which is gone down at the sundial of Ahaz, ten degrees backward. So the sun returned ten degrees, by which degrees it was gone down" (Isaiah 39:8 KJV).

Then we all know of sinners who break every rule in the book, and yet are among the first to be healed in a service. Others who outwardly live godly lives go away as afflicted as when they came. But one must not forget that these are exceptions rather than the rule.

Another factor is that the sinner may seldom, if ever, have attended a Bible-believing church; so he is one to whom little has been given. On the other hand, the unhealed Christian may have gone to church all his life, therefore much is required of him. Often a sinner's healing points to the veracity of Christ's claim to be Savior, since He is both Healer and Savior.

Miracles do happen to those who do not seek for them; and sometimes to those who do not even believe in the supernatural. But they are rare. Personally I would not gamble on the chance that I might be one of those whose healing comes without any obligation on my part as to faith or right living. And if I did not then turn to Christ, I might be blessed with a healed body, but I would still be shackled to a doomed soul.

As further testimony to the rarity of God's exceptions, consider that God has only stopped the sun in its course for one man in all of history. "And there was no day like that before it or after it, that the Lord hearkened unto the voice of a man . . ." (Joshua 10:14 KJV).

If somewhere in the following pages you find a reflection of *your* problem, expose it for what it is—a hindrance to your healing (not something to be coddled, even if it is your pet fancy). Remember, anything that keeps us from God's best is sin. Anything that prevents us from enjoying the health of God has been induced by the enemy of our souls, for he knows that a sick body is no testimony for Christ; neither is it fit for strenuous service for our Lord.

Rise up! Shake off those shackles of bondage! Rid yourself of every hindrance. Dare to believe God for His health. Release your faith. Allow it to soar until you have been caught away into the heavenlies where your healing awaits you.

3

How Can Faith Bring Healing?

". . . because of your faith it will happen" (Matthew 9:29b TLB).

It is no wonder that so many Christians are frustrated in their spiritual experiences. They became Christians by faith, but they have never learned the principles of the walk of faith. Yet "it is impossible to please God without faith" (Hebrews 11:6 JB). They struggle from one crisis to the next, knowing little or nothing of I Peter 5:7—"You can throw the whole weight of your anxieties upon Him, for you are His personal concern" (Phillips). How futile to approach God on any other terms than absolute trust.

Following your conversion, top priority should be given to faith, for it is the requisite for receiving *all* the

20

graces of God. "For whatever does not proceed from faith is sin" (Romans 14:23b RSV). Since we cannot please God without it, a life filled with faith ought to be the primary goal of all Christians.

When that truth becomes operative for *you*, your whole Christian walk will be radically altered for the good. Many have come to treat unbelief as a minor thing, or a thing to be laughed at. Often they make light of their doubts. But doubt is no laughing matter—it is sin!

The Apostle Paul takes us on a magnificent journey as we proceed through the book of Ephesians. We find ourselves walking where angels dwell. But then, Paul brings us plummeting earthward and reminds us that earth is where we live for now. True, we walk in the heavenlies in the Spirit, but we do battle here on this earth. This warfare is not fought in the flesh, but with the weapons of the Spirit.

Paul points out the various parts of a good soldier's armor. All of them add protection, but the most essential piece is the shield of faith. "Above all be sure to take faith as your shield . . ." (Ephesians 6:16 Phillips). In the eyes of God, trusting Him for all of our needs is paramount; and that includes the need to be healed. When we place our faith in Him, we are placing our trust in His resources.

God's resources are so vast. The human mind cannot begin to grasp the height, the breadth and the depth of all that belongs to our heavenly Father. The entire universe is at His disposal. As His children, we can partake of them as we speak the word of faith. Healing abounds—the Bible speaks of it in Ezekiel 47:9 as a river: "And everywhere that river runs, it brings life and health" (KJV). This river shall never run dry. It flows for your healing *right now.*

21

If God lacks the ability to deliver us from sickness, then the claims of Christ were only idle prattle: the ravings of an egomaniac with delusions of grandeur. However, if He is able to fulfill His statements, then we are confronted with power beyond all human understanding! Is He able? Let's consider His record.

"All creation took place through Him, and none took place without Him" (John 1:3 Phillips). This world, the spinning galaxies, the universe—were His creation. He spoke, and they all came into existence. From the dust of the earth He formed man, and breathed into him the breath of life, and man became a living soul.

"Through Him, and for Him, also, were created power and dominion, ownership and authority. In fact, all things were created through, and for Him. He is both the first principle and the upholding principle of the whole scheme of creation" (Colossians 1:16, 17 Phillips). Since God is the "upholding principle" He is able to touch every fragment of that creation. He is able to make your body well and strong.

You also need to believe in His willingness to heal you! It is easy to believe that God will heal other people, but much harder to know that He will heal *you*. The willingness of God to heal all (you included) stands out as a biblical truth.

"Many are the afflictions of the righteous; but the Lord delivereth him out of them all" (Psalm 34:19 KJV)—not some of them, many of them, or most of them—but *all* of them. "Who forgiveth all thine iniquities; who healeth all thy diseases" (Psalm 103:3 KJV). His desire to heal all the sick is as evident as His will to save all men.

"I will put none of these diseases upon thee, which I have brought upon the Egyptians: for I am the Lord that healeth thee" (Exodus 15:26 KJV).

"They will lay their hands upon the sick and they will recover" (Mark 16:18 Phillips). "Believing prayer will save [heal] the sick man" (James 5:15 Phillips). No limitations are set as to who, how many or what sicknesses!

The leper said to Christ, "If you want to, you can make me clean." The Master replied, "Of course I want to . . ." (Mark 1:40 Phillips).

"A man is only as good as his word," the saying goes. That might be paraphrased, "God is only as good as His Word!" If one area of His Word is not trustworthy, then all of His promises become suspect. But this guarantee rests upon His Word. "I will hasten [to stand behind or to protect] my word to perform it" (Jeremiah 1:12 KJV).

Faith is placing one's trust in the word of another, believing that what they have promised they will do. "There hath not failed one word of all His good promises" (I Kings 8:56 KJV). His promises are not bound by the limitations of time and space, as are the agreements of men. "Forever, O Lord, thy word is settled in heaven" (Psalm 119:89 KJV).

"And though all heaven and earth shall pass away, yet my words remain forever true" (Luke 21:33 TLB). By God's very nature, He cannot lie. "God is not a man, that He should lie; neither the son of man, that He should repent: hath He said, and shall He not do it? Or hath He spoken, and shall He not make it good?" (Numbers 23:19 KJV).

"The man who will not believe God is making Him out to be a liar, because he is refusing to accept the testimony that God has given . . ." (I John 5:10 Phillips).

F.F. Bosworth said, "If you're going to doubt anything,

doubt your doubts." They are totally unreliable, whereas the testimony of God has stood the test of time. People believe and trust in their symptoms (their senses) which are often unreliable; yet they will not believe God's Word which has never failed.

If God were to lie even once, He would have to violate His own nature: the truth. But the whole creation attests to His truthfulness. Has God ever failed to keep His Word? He has promised to move heaven and earth, if necessary, to fulfill His promises.

There are many who will not believe that the Lord still heals today. "Miracles were only for the Apostolic Age," they say. "Jesus only healed the sick to prove who He was, and to establish His Church. Afterwards, these displays of power were no longer necessary. His Church has been built and there is no longer any need for miracles and healings."

I remember a service in Fremont, Ohio, in which a four-year-old boy was brought for healing of cerebral palsy. He reached the platform by throwing his little legs, heavy with braces, in awkward arcs. His distorted speech was hardly understandable.

Kneeling in front of Donnie, I looked into his beautiful eyes and asked him what he wanted. Donnie wanted to run and jump and laugh and talk, and to be able to smile at people. But there wasn't anything to smile about.

The small boy spent hours at a window watching other children play and do things that he would never be able to do. Then his family heard about an evangelist named Seavey who prayed for the sick. Many were going away healed of serious diseases. So, with great effort, Donnie's grandmother brought him the one hundred miles to the crusade.

Now he stood before me with tear-filled eyes, wanting "to be like other boys."

I looked deeply into those searching eyes and, with all of the authority of God's Word, I told Donnie that Jesus loved him and wanted to heal him now.

"Is Jesus still able to heal the sick, Donnie?"

"Yes," he quickly answered.

"Do you believe that Jesus will heal you now?"

"Yes, I believe He will."

I suppose that I should have informed Donnie he was theologically wrong—that Jesus doesn't do that any more. I should have said, "Donnie, Jesus healed people only because He wanted to build a large church and that was the only way He could do it. Since we now have the church established, He doesn't need to heal any more." I couldn't say that to Donnie.

I hugged him and began to weep. I couldn't pray words—they wouldn't come. At that moment I began to understand the compassion Jesus has for the sick.

The Compassionate One is *still* "touched with the feelings of our infirmities." That moment Christ's compassion overflowed and the river of healing surged through Donnie's body. Instantly he was made whole. Pushing me aside, he did first the thing he had always wanted to do—run. Around and around that large auditorium he ran, four times!

About a month later his grandmother reported that after arriving home, they had removed his braces. He was now able to live a perfectly normal life, doing everything four-year-old boys do, and "talking a blue streak."

The power and compassion of a loving Savior is revealed in Scripture:

"Jesus went round all the towns and villages . . .

curing every kind of ailment and disease. The sight of the people moved Him to pity" (Matthew 9:35, 36b NEB).

"When He came ashore, He saw a great crowd; His heart went out to them, and He cured those of them who were sick" (Matthew 14:14 NEB).

"Jesus was filled with pity for him, and stretched out His hand and placed it on the leper, saying, of course I want to—*be clean*" (Mark 1:41 Phillips).

When Christ came across the funeral procession at Nain and saw the mother weeping over her only son whom they were about to bury, it is written, "When the Lord saw her, his heart went out to her and He said, *'Don't cry.'* He then proceeded to raise her son to life again" (Luke 7:13 Phillips).

The word *compassion* appears everywhere in the Bible accounts of Jesus healing the sick. His reasons have not changed because He never changes. ". . . His compassions fail not: they are new every morning: great is thy faithfulness" (Lamentations 3:22, 23 KJV).

Reach out right now and allow His compassion to flow down on your sick body. Feel His tender hand of love as He places it gently upon your weary frame. That same unfailing compassion brings health and strength to you.

We have been dealing with the subject of faith, for it is the basis for all healing. God expects faith just as surely as the grocer expects money in return for goods. Certainly it is a small-enough price to pay for our health.

Many are not healed in services because they expect the evangelist to pray the "prayer of faith" for their need. All through the meeting they sit thinking that someone else will do their work for them. Though there are times when someone else prays in faith for one whose faith is weak,

26

this is not the usual plan for healing. God's highest standard for receiving healing has always been the individual exercise of faith. Most of the Lord's healings were not accomplished through His faith (although He had all faith), but rather through the belief of the individual who believed the words that He spoke.

In Matthew we read about two blind men who followed the Lord requesting to be healed. They even followed Him into the house where He was staying. At that point, Jesus asked them, "Do you believe I can make you see? . . . Because of *your faith* it will happen" (Matthew 9: 28,29 TLB).

To the woman who had the issue of blood twelve years He said, "Cheer up, my daughter, *your faith* has made you well" (Matthew 9:22 Phillips).

When Jesus approached His hometown with the Gospel it is written, "And He could do nothing miraculous there, apart from laying His hands upon a few sick people and healing them; their lack of faith astonished Him" (Mark 6:5 Phillips).

In another instance, a blind man had been brought to the Lord for healing. "Then He moistened his eyes with saliva and putting His hands upon him, asked, 'Can you see at all?' The man looked up and said, 'I can see people. They look like trees—only they are walking about.' Then Jesus put His hands on his eyes once more and his sight came into focus, and he recovered, and saw everything sharp and clear" (Mark 8:23b, 25 Phillips).

Obviously, the perfect faith of the Son of God would not have required more than one attempt to bring about absolute and flawless healing for this man, if that were all that was necessary. His healing came about by his own somewhat shaky but improving faith.

To the centurion whose servant was ill, Jesus said, "Go home now; because of *your faith,* so let it be" (Matthew 8:13 NEB).

To the Syrophoenician woman He said, " 'Woman, what *faith* you have! Be it as you wish!' And from that moment her daughter was restored to health" (Matthew 15:28 NEB).

Time and again Jesus stated that the miracle performed was according to the faith of the sufferer, rather than by His own Divine intervention alone. Read: Mark 10:52; Luke 8:48; 17:19; 18:42, 43; Acts 14:19; Matthew 9:27-30; 15:28; Mark 5:34; John 4:47-53—and see for yourself.

While it is possible to be healed through another's faith, God never intended that this should be the normal course of action. The Bible refers to the believer's authority in Christ over sin, sickness and demon powers; and God wants you to begin exercising your spiritual prerogatives. A glorious dawning of faith awaits you when you comprehend the potential that has been locked up within you. *You* are more than a conqueror, *you* are a victor! The devil has no real power over you—neither does sickness and disease! What a keen sense of spiritual exhilaration will sweep over you when you believe God for personal healing and He answers your prayer of faith. Don't wait for an evangelist or pastor to pray the prayer of faith for you; that may never happen. The prayer of another merely assists *our* faith; it does not take the place of it.

Have you wondered why God hasn't healed *you,* while those all about you receive miracles? Perhaps the Lord is waiting for your faith to reach out into His storehouse of healing and take "what ye will." " 'Did I not tell you,' replied Jesus, 'that if you believed, you would see the wonder of what God can do?' " (John 11:40 Phillips).

4

What About the Symptoms?

After following instructions of the Word of God and praying the prayer of faith for our healing, then we trust God's *unchanging* Word which has never failed. Many times people remark that even though they had been prayed for, their pain or swelling or fever continued. "If the pain would only go away," they say, "I could believe I was healed."

Anyone can believe what he sees, but faith believes what it cannot see. Faith sees the invisible. Faith accepts the impossible. Faith appropriates the unobtainable. Faith wins victories against overwhelming odds. Faith lifts the believer over insurmountable obstacles. Faith heals sick bodies.

Man consists of spirit, soul and body. The *body*, man's outer shell, gives him knowledge of his physical surroundings through the senses of taste, touch, smell, sight and hearing. The *spirit* of man exists for the purpose of relating to God. This medium allows man to be conscious of all that is spiritual. The *soul*, which is capable of exercising will, intellect and emotions, acts as the intermediary between the spiritual and the physical.

The fact that man has been endowed with a spirit makes him unique among all of God's creation! A mighty lion or the loftiest bird can not make that claim. They are earthly; while man was made to know God.

Jesus Himself declared, ". . . true worshippers will worship the Father in spirit [their spirits] and in reality . . . God is Spirit, and those who worship Him can only worship in spirit and in reality" (John 4:23, 24 Phillips).

In the Old Testament God commanded Moses to make a tabernacle (a large, portable tent) which would be the center of worship for the Jews as they wandered through the wilderness. A high, white linen fence surrounded this tent and formed a large courtyard. The Tabernacle was divided into two sections: the holy place and the innermost sanctuary, the Holy of Holies.

The outer court with its altar of sacrifice represents man's flesh and Christ's atonement for sin on Calvary.

The holy place, situated between the outer court and the Holy of Holies, symbolized man's soul—the bridge between the flesh and the spirit.

However, it was not in the outer court or even in the holy place that God met with man. Exodus 25 describes the design and furnishings of the Holy of Holies. God said to Moses in verse twenty-two: "And there I will meet with thee, and I will commune with thee from above the mercy

30

seat . . ." (KJV) The Holy of Holies typifies the spirit of man, his innermost sanctuary. God has declared that all true worship must find its origination in man's spirit. Since God is Spirit and has designed that true worship originates in the spirit of man, it is on this plane that "deep calleth unto deep . . ." (Psalm 42:7 KJV). Man's innermost recess reaches out to the sanctuary of God's Spirit, and there a holy union is formed.

The soul is linked to the world through the bodily senses. But the spirit of man is linked to God, bringing about a spiritual union. Scripture makes it clear that the flesh and the Spirit realms are not wholly compatible.

For example, as I write this I sit at my desk by a window overlooking Wisconsin's beautiful Lake Delavan. A hundred feet away stands a stately, old weeping willow tree. Just beyond the tree, a boat is tied to the landing slip, rocking gently on the waves. The majestic hills stand sentry over the lake.

My eyes take in all this vast panorama of beauty, but I ask, "Is there more? Am I missing something that's really there, which I simply can't see with these eyes?"

The answer, of course, is *yes*. These eyes were not made to see into the realm of the spirit. Neither were my other four senses created to experience by themselves that realm of spirit in which heavenly beings live.

Then exactly what is there in my surroundings that I seem to be missing with my natural vision? I am convinced that if my spiritual vision were opened, I would see the angels of God surrounding me. Also present might be some forces of evil bent on destroying this book which will help many to receive healing. I might actually behold quite a battle going on in front of that tranquil lake—*if* I could only see into the realm of the spirit.

A rather amusing story in Scripture (II Kings 6) illustrates this point. The king of Syria and his entire army surrounded the house of the Prophet Elisha. They were eager to destroy Elisha for having forewarned the king of Israel of Syria's battle plans made in secret, but revealed to the prophet by the Spirit of God.

"And when the servant of the man of God was risen early, and gone forth, behold, an host compassed the city both with horses and chariots. And his servant said unto him, Alas, my master! How shall we do? And he answered, Fear not: for they that be with us are more than they that be with them. And Elisha prayed, and said, Lord, I pray thee, open his eyes, that he may see. And the Lord opened the eyes of the young man; and he saw: and behold, the mountain was full of horses and chariots of fire round about Elisha."

Those angelic hosts didn't *just* appear, they had been there all along. Elisha had grown so sensitive to the things of the Spirit that he was immediately aware of their presence. His servant Gehazi focused on the Syrian army, and thought the end for both of them was near at hand.

Consider what a strange prayer the prophet prayed for Gehazi—that his eyes might be *opened*. But wasn't it Gehazi who had brought the devastating news to Elisha that the Syrian armies were gathered all over the hillsides? There was nothing wrong with his eyesight. Elisha wasn't concerned about his physical vision. The prophet prayed that the inner eyes of the spirit would be illuminated.

There were angels to be seen, with chariots and horses of fire. Gehazi would have missed it all if his inner eyes had not been opened by the Spirit of God. But even had he been totally blind to that great battle, that would not have affected what was happening. The fact that we can't see the guardian angels who protect us daily does not negate their presence. "But the unspiritual man simply cannot accept the matters which the Spirit deals with—they just don't make sense to him, for after all, you must be spiritual to see spiritual things" (I Corinthians 2:14 Phillips).

Consequently, it seems ludicrous to some, while symptoms remain, to deny actual pain or abnormalities and believe they are healed.

"I am the Lord that healeth thee" (Exodus 15:26 KJV).

"They shall lay hands on the sick, and they shall recover" (Mark 16:18 KJV).

Every promise of healing is in the absolutely positive sense. Faith is an exercise of the spirit of man, which believes that what God has promised He will perform. Faith grasps the promises of the Word and holds on to them until they become a physical reality.

"Now faith is the substance of things hoped for, the evidence of things not seen" (Hebrews 11:1 KJV).

Seeing an optical illusion can be a frustrating experience. Our senses register one thing while reality is something else altogether. Being a pilot, I often enjoy taking a friend up for a flight. After awhile I ask him to close his eyes. While his eyes remain closed, I gently ease the plane into a steep bank.

"What do you think our angle of flight is?"

Almost invariably he answers, "straight and level."

Imagine the look of amazement when he opens his eyes and finds himself seated at a 45-degree angle! One of the first lessons in flight training drill is: don't trust your senses; they are unreliable. Believe the instruments

33

because they have been made to measure what the senses cannot.

That lesson also applies to healing. Your spirit is able to sense what is happening in the realm of God's Spirit—even if you are mentally unaware of it. It is not a strange thing to speak of having been healed even while the symptoms persist, because faith takes the Word of God at face value, believes and appropriates it even though the outward signs in the flesh indicate something entirely different.

Remember the last time you saw a bumblebee? What was he doing? Flying? That's interesting, because the bumblebee *can't fly.*

According to aerotechnical tests, it is impossible for the bumblebee to fly. The shape of its body is aerodynamically unsuited for flight. Its overall body weight is far in excess of what its wings can support. And, even if its wings were strong enough to support it, the bee can't move them fast enough to sustain lift. Of course, the bumblebee doesn't know this, so he just goes ahead and flies.

The laws of flight say that it can't be done. These facts were deduced by men who have all the knowledge of physics and flight at their disposal. The bumblebee can't fly—that's logic! Man's logic *is* often limited and untrue.

The example of Abraham and Sarah also illustrates this concept of faith without sight. God promised Abraham that He would give him a son. Many years passed but no physical evidence indicated that the promise would be fulfilled. When Abram (which means "blessed father") approached his one hundredth birthday, God changed his name to Abraham—"father of many nations!" The time for childbearing had long passed for ninety-year-old

Sarah. Logically, no hope of fulfilling that promise existed.

"Abraham, when hope was dead within him, went on hoping in faith, believing that he would become 'the father of many nations.' He relied on the Word of God, which definitely referred to 'thy seed.' With undaunted faith he looked at the facts—his own impotence (he was practically a hundred years old at the time) and his wife Sarah's apparent barrenness. Yet he refused to allow any distrust of a definite pronouncement of God to make him waver. He . . . remained absolutely convinced that God was able to implement His own promise" (Romans 4:18-21 Phillips).

Like Abraham, faith sees the symptoms but accepts the Word of God as final. If God's Word says that you *are* healed, then that is final and you can rest in its assurance.

"Can I *never* believe my senses?" you may ask. "Are they to be completely ignored?"

Certainly your senses may be relied upon as long as they align themselves with the will of God. When they contradict the Scriptures, then you must believe God's testimony rather than that of the flesh.

The natural man sees a ravaging illness taking its toll upon some hapless victim. Faith sees that same person healthy and strong. The natural man hears the doctor's prognosis that there is "no hope." Faith hears the voice of the Spirit saying, "All is well." The natural man feels the gnawing pain of cancer as it destroys his body, but faith feels divine health and strength flowing in the spirit.

My father deserted our family when I was only seven. Life was difficult but we were a close-knit unit—at least we had each other.

What About the Symptoms?

Eight years later, an extremely black period descended over our family. My mother began to experience pain in her spine. At first, massaging her back gave relief. But soon, the pain increased in intensity and frequency. A doctor was consulted. X-rays were taken. The diagnosis was crippling osteo-arthritis.

This disease progressed rapidly over the next several months, twisting Mom's spine into the shape of a "lazy S." Her neck was bent out of shape until her head rested on her shoulder. Large deposits of calcium built up on her spinal column in great, ugly lumps. Medical science had no real hope to offer her—only a metal brace to hold her stooped frame erect. This caused more pain, and Mom could never wear it without crying.

Seeking relief, she began to visit a chiropractor. I would often escort her to his office and wait for her. Having grown up without a father in the tough environment of Brooklyn, I was not "soft." Yet for all my toughness, I could not bear my mother's anguished screams coming from the treatment room. Helplessly, I walked the street outside, weeping as I waited for her treatments to end.

When her chiropractor learned that Mom had been given a steel brace by the medical doctor, he was alarmed. His prognosis was grim: at the rate her arthritis was progressing, she would be in a wheelchair permanently within five years, certainly no longer. But if she continued to wear the brace, he could do nothing for her and she would be crippled much sooner.

Mom went back to her medical doctor, thinking he might have more optimistic news for her. But the picture he painted was no brighter. He related the same story—only in reverse. He told her if she continued to visit the chiropractor and refused to wear her brace she would be hopelessly crippled in short order—her only hope was that brace.

Only one point of agreement existed between the doctor and the chiropractor: the *most* time she could expect before being confined to a wheelchair as a hopelessly twisted cripple was five years.

At that time, our family knew nothing of divine healing. In fact, even salvation was a rather new experience for us. But in her desperation, my mother made two spiritual pilgrimages. She visited shrines, hoping for some improvement, but returned disappointed and frustrated.

Her pain became almost intolerable. She was confined to her bed for relief, what little she could find. When Mom stood, she could no longer straighten her back or stand upright. She was embarrassed to go anywhere, especially where people knew her.

You can imagine my surprise when she asked to be taken to church one Sunday morning. It was a major undertaking to get her into and out of the car, and greater effort to get her into the church. The eight steps leading into the building might as well have been eight hundred—even one step was a monumental obstacle. We would have carried her, had there been a way, but the pain would have been unbearable. So we waited and watched her drag that grotesquely twisted body up those eight steps.

She suffered great pain every moment of that service. Though much of the sermon was unintelligible because of her agony, one thing the minister said stood out like a beaconlight.

"Jesus Christ is the Great Physician. What is not possible with man *is* possible with God."

Then, deep within, a voice spoke to my mother saying, "I have healed you. In three weeks' time you will be well."

Surprisingly, for someone who had never learned the things of the Spirit, Mom believed without hesitation. She knew that the work was already done . . . she was healed!

The service ended and the benediction was pronounced. But there she was—still twisted and deformed. The pain was even greater from having sat through a one-hour service on a hard, wooden pew.

But there was a difference! She had received a word from God. Deep inside her was the assurance of the Holy Spirit's words, "I have healed you!" Although both the medical and chiropractic professions gave her little time left to walk, now she had received another, more professional opinion from The Great Physician.

The following day her sister Millie arrived to drive her for treatment. The choice must be made—to wear or not to wear the brace. Millie looked bewildered when Mom announced that she had heard a voice tell her that she was healed.

"Well, if you *are* healed," Aunt Millie answered, "then how come you're not walking and your body is still twisted? If you don't come for treatment, I'll not be responsible for you when you're all crippled."

Mom had already made her decision. All that remained was to wait the appointed three weeks. Every day seemed to contain forty-eight hours. The symptoms mocked her belief that she had been healed. There was not one outward sign to testify of any change in her body. She even felt worse at times.

As the days passed, many of those close to us heard of Mom's belief and thought the strain had broken her mind.

If she were already straightened, that would have been *proof* to them; to believe what was obviously not true seemed ludicrous. But never once did Mom's faith waver during those three trying weeks.

The night before the three-week period ended Mom was not even slightly better. It would have been so easy to change her mind and confess that she had been overly enthusiastic, that the voice had been a product of her own subconscious mind. After all, sickness does do some strange things to people who have suffered for long periods. No one would have held it against her. But Mom wasn't having any of that! God had said she was already healed and that she would be straight in three weeks' time. Tomorrow morning would be the crucial moment.

Sleep came that night, but not easily. How would it happen? When would it happen? What would it be like when she became straight? What would it feel like? Strangely enough, Mom would never know the "hows" or the "whens," nor could she even explain what it felt like when the Lord took her twisted body and made it straight.

When she awoke the next morning there was not a twisted bone in her body. The spinal curvature was gone. Her neck was straight and the large calcium deposits had disappeared from her vertebrae. For the first time in over a year she was able to get out of bed by herself and stand upright—no canes, no brace, no pain, and no crippling arthritis!

That happened twenty-three years ago, and she has never had a trace of these problems since. When asked to comment, Mom simply says, "I'm glad I listened to the voice of God rather than to my symptoms. Had I listened to them, I would be a hopeless cripple today instead of a strong and healthy person."

What About the Symptoms?

We cannot understand spiritual things with a mind geared to the natural realm. The man of the flesh lives in constant servitude to circumstances, while the man of faith *makes things happen*. When the man of the flesh, taken with some dread disease, resigns himself to die, the man of faith, faced with the same disease, designs great plans for the future. The difference is found in their sense of sight. The natural eye was only made to see as far as the flesh. Faith, with the eye of the Spirit, sees what God can do.

When Gehazi, the Prophet Elisha's servant, saw the Syrian horses, chariots and soldiers which had come to capture Elisha, he reported what he had seen to Elisha who remained undisturbed. He didn't ignore the Syrians, but he saw beyond them. There stood the armies of heaven ready to defend and preserve him.

Faith denies everything that is out of alignment with the Word of God. Your sickness, if you are a child of God, is out of alignment with His promises: "The prayer of faith shall heal the sick, and the Lord shall raise him up." And again, ". . . they shall recover," says the Word of God. Will you decide to step out—not upon the precarious footing of your senses, but upon the firm foundation of *faith* in God's Word? Believe that you are healed because the Bible says so, and you will see it come to pass!

5

When Is Healing Not a Miracle?

Millions of people have passed through prayer lines for the sick, only to leave disappointed and unhealed. Why? There is no single answer for this perplexing question.

While in prayer, the Holy Spirit spoke very clearly to me, and answered part of the question: There is a difference between *healings* and *miracles*.

I Corinthians mentions nine gifts of the Holy Spirit, given for the edification of the Church. One is the gift of miracles. Healing is mentioned as a separate gift. The word *healing* carries with it the connotation of an action which occurs over a period of time. A miracle happens instantaneously. If God had intended for every person's symptoms to vanish immediately after prayer—a mira-

41

cle—there would be no need for the gift of healing.

Our bodies are a miracle in themselves. The Psalmist exclaimed, "I will praise thee; for I am fearfully and wonderfully made" (Psalm 139:14 KJV). Our bodies were never made to be sick! God created our bodies to fight off the attack of invading germs. Healing is the natural process. However, we can lower our bodies' resistance to germs through overwork, unbridled appetites, or other excesses, and sickness results.

Doctors will admit that neither they nor their medicine can heal the sick. To prove this, place some medicine and a bandage on the wound of a dead man. Upon later inspection, you will find that the wound is unchanged. The healing essence of life (which comes from God) no longer exists. All the skill and medication in the world cannot cure, no matter how well applied. Medical science merely *assists* our bodies in their natural healing function.

It may *kill the invading germs*, but it does not heal the body. Once the germs have been destroyed, the body then goes about its curative work of restoration, and we recover. Medication may *supply additives* missing in the diet that are necessary to health. This allows the body to carry on its normal functions and perform properly.

Then there is surgery, where a portion of the affected area is *removed*. This can hardly be considered a healing, because if the body does not recover from the effects of the surgery, death will result. Medical science is not directly responsible for healing. It *is* an assistance to nature which God created.

Illness indicates that the physical mechanism simply isn't doing its job right. This is where the gift of healing enters the scene. Mark 16:18b (Jerusalem Bible) states: "They will lay their hands upon the sick, who will recover." No immediate cessation of all symptoms is promised, but that a curative process would begin. The laying-on of hands in this instance is akin to the application of medicine, which brings about a *process* of healing from that moment on.

When someone is prayed for and their affliction leaves instantaneously, then we have seen the gift of miracles in action. We have witnessed a *healing miracle*. Of course, it is true that whatever God does is a miracle. If His touch takes the place of medicine and hospital care, I see this as a great miracle, even if the person prayed for doesn't see a total turnabout of their symptoms in a split second of time. I have learned never to minimize *any* work of the Holy Spirit.

Since the promise is, "They will lay their hands on the sick, who will recover," how is it that so many who have submitted to this rite are not healed?

For many, the laying on of hands is nothing more than a religious ritual. All of the promises of God are appropriated by faith, not by ritual. You must remember that these signs follow "them that believe." That may literally be translated not only the followers, but "those who will have faith for the signs." The promises of God have always been "to them that believe." No one can come to the altar as a ritual for salvation and expect to go away saved. If the laying-on of hands diminishes into ritual we shouldn't expect to receive healing. It simply doesn't work that way.

Most Christians don't differentiate between *miracles* and *healings*. When they go forward for prayer, they are instinctively looking for a miracle of healing. When it doesn't happen, they become disappointed.

How often have you heard someone ask a friend who

43

had just been prayed for: "How do you feel now?"

And they reply, "Well, I guess this just wasn't my time to be healed, because I've still got my symptoms."

Do you see what is taking place at that moment? They are confessing their sickness, their symptoms, their pain, rather than confessing what the Word of God says: "They will lay their hands on the sick, who *will* recover." They are believing their symptoms instead of God.

Several months ago I began to feel discomfort between my shoulder blades at the base of my neck. At first, I simply dismissed it as a side-effect of a rigorous schedule of traveling, preaching and ministering to the sick. *Naturally my muscles and joints would tighten up,* I thought.

Then one day a small lump appeared, not much bigger than a pea. I convinced myself that it was nothing to be concerned about, and casually brushed aside my wife's admonition to "have that seen to."

The days slipped by into weeks. The small lump grew half as large as a hen's egg, accompanied by pains radiating out to my right shoulder joint and up my neck. I prayed for a miracle to take place. More than once I found myself thinking about the prospect of cancer and an untimely death.

The weeks became months with no sign of relief. Awaking one morning with more than the usual degree of pain, I touched the tumor and found it larger than the day before and inflamed with fever. That did it. Indignation arose within me and in faith I commanded the tumor to go in the name of Jesus. I clung to the promise in the Word of God: "They shall lay hands on the sick, and they shall recover."

Can you imagine what happened at that dramatic moment? Nothing. That's right—*nothing.* At least that's what natural reasoning would have had me believe—but I knew that the work was accomplished. My healing was assured by the word of the living God.

Each day I would reach around the back of my neck and place my hand upon the tumor to see what progress my faith was making. For over a week I could detect no discernable change in either its size or in my pain.

One morning in particular as I found both the size of the growth and the pain to be no different from several days before. I laughed out loud and said: "Tumor, you may not realize it yet, but you *have* to go. The Word of God says, 'they shall lay hands on the sick, and they shall recover.' I will not believe what my natural senses tell me—I believe the Word of the Lord."

From that morning on, my healing could be visibly measured. Over the next six weeks that tumor lost its grip on my body and finally dissolved. Today not a trace of it remains; I'm healed completely.

If you will speak the language of faith, you will find it never goes unrewarded. Believe that as hands are placed upon you, your healing *begins* at that instant. Many have lost what God began to do for them, because they looked for an instant miracle. I don't mean that you shouldn't hope for a miracle, but if it doesn't happen, go on believing in what God has done.

What I've written hasn't been with an eye to discourage faith, as some might suppose, but to present an adjunct to it. Since that day when the Holy Spirit spoke this to me, I have preached it in many parts of the world and have found a warm reception to this truth. Now, when I return to cities where I've preached, I find exuberant people who have since applied it and, as a consequence, have been healed, *gradually*.

When Is Healing Not a Miracle?

One lady in Orchard Park, New York, told me that she had been prayed for so often over the five years of her illness, that she had begun to despair of ever being well again. When she didn't receive an instantaneous miracle for her kidney disease, she thought she had received nothing; and she got what she believed for—nothing. After hearing me preach this truth, she applied it to her case and her health began to improve from that moment on. She now enjoys perfect health with no trace of a kidney disorder.

Why not believe God right now? Lay hands on your own body and pray for your recovery.

"Am I able to do this?" you may ask.

Are you a believer? Then of course you may, for these signs are to follow *you*. Believe that as *you* comply with God's Word, He will honor it, and health shall begin to spring forth. New strength will be yours—beginning now!

6

Is It God's Will This Time?

To be healed, we are instructed to pray the *prayer of faith;* not to simply recite words, nor to beg and plead, nor to "make a deal" with God. Pray in faith, and believe that what we have requested is on the way. The great faith-destroying phrase is: "If it be Thy will." Many Christians believe that this is the humble way to approach God for health.

After all, you must be very careful how you approach God. You don't want to be too presumptuous. Tread gently now and ask 'If it be Thy will,' for who are you to pretend to know the will of God? Nonsense!

The word "if" presupposes *doubt* and uncertainty concerning the will of God; whereas *faith* speaks with an authority that is born from above. Faith is the language of God learned from the study of His Word.

The section of the Bible called the New Testament actually means "new will." If we want to know what Uncle Harry left us in his will, the obvious course of action would be to obtain a copy of the will and read it!

Every one of us has an available copy of the will of God: His Word.

God has made it abundantly clear that it is His will to heal all who come to Him in faith. There is no reason why we should ever approach the subject of healing with uncertainty. God's will to heal all is as clearcut in His Word as His will to save everyone. Both are not only reflected in what He said but also by what He did. His promises to heal are as valid today as His promises to save. If I cannot believe the Scriptures which teach that healing is in effect now, then I have grounds upon which to doubt my salvation.

Not *one* reference in Scripture verifies that God has withdrawn any of His New Will promises. His will has always been to heal the sufferings of humanity, and God never changes. He is *still* "the Lord that healeth thee" (Exodus 15:26 KJV). Every time Jesus healed, He revealed the will of God to men. He came to do the will of the Father.

There are Christians who believe that it is the will of God for them to be sick. They argue that it is wrong for us to pray for divine healing because "God is working out some deep work of grace in the sufferer's life." However, they hurry to a doctor for medication in order to be healed. Incongruous, isn't it? If sickness is the will of God, why undertake to remove it by any means, medical or otherwise?

48

If this has been your block against divine healing, Satan has blinded your eyes to the healing that is yours. He is a liar and the father of all lies. See him for what he is, and then take a new look at the Word of God. I am certain you will reach the obvious conclusion: God wants to heal *you*—now!

"My prayer for you, my very dear friend, is that you may be as healthy and prosperous in every way as you are in soul" (III John 2 Phillips).

"We can approach God with confidence [faith] for this reason: if we make requests which accord with His will He listens to us; and if we know that our requests are heard, we know also that the things we ask for are ours" (I John 5:14,15 NEB).

You can learn to pray with that kind of certainty for your healing once you have become convinced that all of the New Will is still in force.

You may say, "But my pastor says that miracles were only for the Apostolic age, and we can't expect healing today."

Ask Him for *one* clear-cut, *scriptural* proof of that statement. Search as he might, there is *not one* reference to God having changed His Will concerning healing! You have every right to be wary of any man who would attempt to change anyone's last will and testament, especially our Lord's. "I am the Lord," He said, "I change not" (Malachi 3:6 KJV). So if any changes have been made, they have not been made by God but by man.

The story is told of a young man walking down the street, carrying a very thin black book under his arm, who was met by a Christian friend.

"It's so good to see you are carrying your New Testament," she said.

"It's not a New Testament," he replied. "It's my Bible."

"Why, that's impossible," said the lady. "It's much too thin to be a whole Bible."

"You see," he explained, "I take it to church with me every Sunday. Every time the preacher reads a portion and then says, 'That's not for today,' I tear out that page. This is all I have left."

Read your New Testament through carefully and underline each reference to healing. You will be amazed at how many Scriptures there are.

After reading His Last Will, you know that healing is in effect today. Now you can pray the prayer of faith. We also know that He will answer us if we pray in accordance with His will, and it *is* the will of God to heal you. Never again pray that faith-destroying phrase, "If it be Thy will." Pray rather, "I *know* it is Thy will to make me well."

7

Do You Really Want to Get Well?

It's an awful thing to be so ill that your body aches or a fever rages; or your limbs are twisted and useless; or you suffer loss of sight or hearing. Christ confronted similar needs almost every day of His ministry. People pressed in upon Him hoping to grasp His garment or to touch His fingertips. Within the crowd of suffering men and women who sought Jesus, every conceivable human need was represented.

Jesus asked many questions of His inquirers, but one seems rather puzzling. "When Jesus saw him lying there on his back—knowing that he had been like that for a long time, He said to him, '*Do you want to get well again?*' " (John 5:6 Phillips).

51

This man to whom Jesus spoke had been ill for thirty-eight years, and from all indications he was a paralytic. Thirty-eight years is a long time to suffer with any ailment, let alone something so debilitating. Why then did Jesus ask, "Do you want to get well again?" Of course he did—wouldn't anyone who was sick?

After years of ministry, I have come to regard that question as one of the most perceptive Jesus ever asked. Some people simply do not want to recover, and never will recover as long as they retain that attitude. Those in the medical profession know the value of "the will to live" if a patient is to survive some critical ailment.

Why would anyone desire to remain paralyzed, crippled, blind or sick with any disease, however great or small? They may enjoy the attention their sickness brings them. Possibly, they are the center of attention at prayer meeting. They monopolize the energies of the pastor who must regularly visit them. In some cases a convenient disability enables the lazy man to do less than his share of work. I know of one man who said, "But if I got healed, I'd lose my disability pension."

These are people who *enjoy* misery. The psychological term for this is *masochism* (to derive a warped sense of pleasure and importance from pain or discomfort). Some even believe they "suffer for the Lord."

In my travels I have visited some monasteries, many of them quite ancient. On one tour the guide led us through what seemed to be a prison cell. Hanging on the wall were long leather cords with jagged pieces of metal affixed to the ends. Other torture devices filled the room. A monk had used these to inflict pain upon himself, in order to find extra favor with God. Often he failed to respond to a call in the morning and would be found on the floor of his cell with his back torn and bleeding. He had whipped himself unconscious.

While visiting an ancient convent I heard that the nuns had slept on bare wooden slats with a piece of wood for a pillow. The explanation was that they had chosen to suffer pain and discomfort for the Lord.

I have watched religious processions where the devout have crawled miles until their knees were reduced to bloody pulp, imbedded with pebbles and sand. This was done in order "to share in the sufferings of our Lord and to obtain special grace and favor." These devout people had no physical afflictions to suffer "for God," so they created some.

I've also met those who were afraid to be healed, because it would alter their entire lifestyle. They refused even to be prayed for.

While conducting a tour of Israel, I met a pleasant gentleman who was totally blind. Our fellowship was warm and friendly, and over the ten days we got to know each other very well.

I asked him, "Since you can't see, what made you want to tour Israel?"

"As my friend here describes the 'sights,' " he replied, "I *feel* them in a way that I cannot explain."

It was only after our friendship was firmly established that I felt free to talk to him about the possibility that God could heal him. We discussed his condition and I learned that he had been injured as a young man when dynamite exploded in his hands, severing most of his fingers and leaving him blind.

"Do you believe God is able to heal you?" I asked.

"Of course He can," he replied, "there's nothing too hard for the Lord."

This man had plenty of faith in God's ability to heal. The difficulty was in his refusal to let God heal him. He did not want to be prayed for! He did not want to be healed! He was quite emphatic.

"When I was younger, before my accident," he related, "I never knew what it was to have any real friends. I ran with a crowd of 'fair-weather friends' who deserted me when I needed them. They could never be depended on. This was very evident when my accident took place. Where were my 'friends' when I needed them to visit me and comfort me? The world of sight had disappeared in a moment of time with a flash of dynamite and, obviously, so had my friends."

At this time of crisis some people from a local church heard about his disaster and came to speak to him about the Lord. Their love and concern for him, combined with the tragedy of the moment, were the elements that led him to commit his life to Christ.

From that moment on he was practically "adopted" by these Christians, who began to do everything for him. He became their ward; living with them, being watched over day and night, led around by the hand like a child. He related this attention and love to his blindness, and over the years had continued to do so. Even in Israel he had a friend to cling to as his personal guide.

"Never before in all my life have I ever known such wonderful friends," he said. "If my sight were to return, they might not be the same to me. I might lose my friends."

What a pity! True, if he regained his sight, he would lose their continual solicitude, but certainly not their friendship. He could not distinguish between the two in his own mind. The old proverb rings true: "There is no one so blind as the man who does not want to see!"

A pastor I know and his friend were at a shopping plaza handing out crusade flyers, when they noticed a pathetic sight. A man crippled from his waist down, struggled to transfer his wheelchair from his car to the pavement. Then with agonizing effort he opened it. Using all his strength, he heaved himself from the seat of the car to the waiting chair. He quickly, but politely, refused an offer of help.

"I'm accustomed to these inconveniences," he explained.

At that moment, a burden for this man's healing came over the pastor. Handing the man a flyer, the pastor extended an invitation to attend the crusade and be prayed for, assuring him that God would heal him if he came.

"I am a Christian," the young man answered. "I love the Lord Jesus with all my heart. In fact, it was this affliction that caused my conversion. Before my disability I was running from God, ignoring anything to do with salvation. Then disaster hit, but with it came the realization that I needed God. In coming face to face with myself, I recognized that I was a sinner in need of a Savior. Accepting forgiveness of sins filled me with joy and peace.

"You see," he concluded, "this crippling was the very means through which I was forced to seek God, and gain salvation. My disability means so much to me because of what it brought. I wouldn't take anything for my crippled legs!"

This Christian associated his disability with his salvation and developed a sentimental attachment to it. He considered the two integral parts of a whole experience. He cultivated a fondness for his condition, going to great lengths to defend it. It was as though his illness had somehow "bought" his salvation, and without it he might lose his relationship with Christ.

How wise was Jesus' question: "Do you *want* to get well again?"

There is only one solution to the problem of hanging on to our sickness. It applies to all who are ill. We must have a clear-cut concept of sickness and its source.

When God created Adam and Eve in the Garden of Eden, He made them perfect in every respect. Neither sin nor sickness could mar them. It wasn't until sin entered their lives that sickness came. All sickness then is the result of evil. I am not suggesting that all persons who are ill have sinned and caused their illness, but that all sickness has evil roots which reach back to the fall of man. Sickness has its origin in Satan. "The thief comes only to steal, to kill and to destroy . . ." (John 10:10 Phillips). Christ came to destroy the works of the enemy by healing the sick.

Concerning the lady who was unable to straighten up for eighteen years, Jesus said: "And here is this woman, a daughter of Abraham, who has been kept prisoner by Satan for eighteen long years . . ." (Luke 13:16 NEB).

When we recognize the cesspool from which all sickness issues, and know that we are permitting Satan to keep his claws in us by remaining sick, then perhaps we will be willing to give it up. Christ has come to set the captives free! Now is the time to break loose from the self-pity in which you have been wallowing, and enjoy the freedom the Holy Spirit brings.

How does someone change long-standing patterns of living? Is there a way to begin thinking right in order to receive healing? The answer has been given to us by the Psalmist: "Delight thyself also in the Lord; and He shall give thee the desires of thine heart" (Psalms 37:4 KJV).

The secret is to delight ourselves in the Lord; that is, to be absolutely wrapped up in the love of God; to find our joy in Him; to love Him with all our hearts and give Him precedence in our lives. We reach this position only through a growth process, but this process does not begin unless we will to move in that direction. Once we have come to that place of total commitment the Bible declares that, "He shall give thee the desires of thine heart."

I do not believe that the Lord will give us whatever we want. However, when we are prepared to abandon ourselves to Him, He will literally put the desires in our hearts that we ought to have. And, since He puts them there, He will grant them!

Stop meditating upon your *sickness.* "But they that wait [meditate] upon the Lord shall renew their strength . . ." (Isaiah 40:31 KJV). Focus your mind upon the promises of God.

"And now, my friends, all that is true, all that is noble, all that is just and pure, all that is lovable and gracious, whatever is excellent and admirable—fill all your thoughts with these things" (Philippians 4:8 NEB). Get rid of those defeatist thoughts and start fresh. Fill your thoughts with the wholesomeness of the mind of Christ. Try to think as He thought. Your healing cannot be far behind.

"When Jesus saw him lying there on his back—knowing that he had been like that for a long time, He said to him, 'Do you want to get well again? . . . Get up . . . pick up your bed and walk!' " (John 5:6,8 Phillips).

8

What Are Your Motives?

Why do some people never receive their healings, although they've been ill for a long time and are prayed for frequently? The answer might be found in diagnosing the motive that prompts their seeking. *Why* are they asking for healing?

"You don't get what you want because you don't ask God for it. And when you do ask He doesn't give it to you, for you ask in quite the wrong spirit—you only want to satisfy your own desires" (James 4:2,3 Phillips).

We can't fully know another's motives for wanting restored health, but God can.

The Bible clearly states that there are times when our prayers aren't answered simply because our motives are wrong in the sight of the Lord. "For man looketh upon the outward appearance, but the Lord looketh on the heart" (I Samuel 16:7 KJV).

I knew a young lady some years ago who couldn't walk. She came for prayer but was not healed. At first I saw a sincere girl who had been refused healing and wondered why. Then I learned what God knew: the primary reason she wanted to be healed (there are usually several reasons for someone to desire healing) was so she could spend her time going deeper into sin. Knowing this would corrupt her, God refused to heal her.

Another time I was praying for the sick when a man laboring to breathe came before me. His difficulty in breathing was so pronounced I found myself wishing I could breathe for him.

"Why do you want to be healed tonight?" I asked.

"Ever since I developed emphysema the doctor made me quit smoking," he replied without hesitation. "He says that if I continue to smoke it will kill me. I miss my cigarets *so* much. If God would heal me it would feel so good to smoke again."

I was shocked. The very habit that had caused this man to contract a potentially fatal disease was the first thing he would return to if healed.

On another occasion, a man informed me that his doctor had forbidden the use of alcohol. He suffered with sclerosis of the liver, and to continue drinking in any quantity was signing his own death warrant. He told me that as soon as he was healed, he would go out and get "a good, stiff drink." Had I heard correctly?

"What did you say?" I asked.

"I'm going to go out and get a good, stiff drink!"

Since both of these men were motivated by wrong

59

desires, neither of them received their healing.

Jesus was concerned about the motivations of the people He healed. He issued a stern warning to the paralytic at the Pool of Bethesda: "Now you are well again, be sure not to sin any more, or something worse may happen to you" (John 5:14b JB).

The Lord knew our human nature—the natural man leans away from God toward the things of the world. You may continue to plead your cause to God over and over. By sheer persistence, you may receive your desires, usually to your detriment, even though you have not complied with His requests.

When a person requests healing, he must make every legitimate effort to live a life pleasing in the sight of the Lord. He treads on thin ice to do otherwise. To receive the blessings of healing from the hand of God, your heart should *first* be right with the Lord.

When an unclean spirit goes out of a man, it wanders through waterless country looking for a place to rest, and cannot find one. Then it says, "I will return to the home I came from." But on arrival, finding it unoccupied, swept and tidied, it then goes off and collects seven other spirits more evil than itself, and they go in and set up house there, so that the man ends up by being worse than he was before.

(Matthew 12:43-45 JB)

Not only is it vitally important that our motives for wanting healing are correct, but we must maintain proper attitudes *after* receiving healing from the hand of God. That Scripture from Matthew implies that the man [home] had been delivered (the evil spirit had gone out). However, he remained neutral toward the things of God. His house (heart and life) was neat and tidy—but empty.

God's Spirit didn't fill the home as an alternative to the departed demonic spirit. He left a welcome mat for trouble—and it moved right in. Trouble seven times worse than he had ever had before. That man would have been better off had he never been helped.

That young lady who was seeking healing of her paralysis, subsequently was healed after she gave her heart to Christ. Shortly thereafter she slipped back into her previous lifestyle of loose morals. Within a year she died of cancer. This wasn't God's plan for her life, but she wouldn't heed His warnings. She paid a heavy price. How unnecessary! If we only listen to the voice of God as revealed in His Word, we appropriate all His promises and enjoy the blessings of His perfect health.

"He will fulfill the desire of them that fear Him: He also will hear their cry, and will save [heal] them" (Psalm 145:19 KJV).

". . . The desire of the righteous shall be granted" (Proverbs 10:24b KJV).

"The desire of the righteous is only good" (Proverbs 11:23 KJV).

Check your motives, and if you find everything in divine order, then press on and claim what is rightfully yours.

9

Temple Keeping

Don't you realize that you yourselves are the temple of God, and that God's Spirit lives in you? God will destroy anyone who defiles His temple, for His temple is holy—and that is exactly what you are!

(I Corinthians 3:16,17 Phillips)

Health balances delicately on the physical, mental, emotional, dietary and spiritual facets of man's life. A strong interaction exists between each component part of man. This interrelatedness makes it difficult to state categorically that any one part is the seat of some physical ailment.

Acute stress can, and often does, cause ulcers, migraine headaches, asthma and a host of other unpleasant side-effects. It is easy to see how the body is influenced even by the way we think.

God *is* a worker of miracles; there is no sickness known to man or yet to be discovered that He cannot heal. However, I am convinced that it is unfair for us to wait upon God for healing when we are contributing to our illness. Let me illustrate.

Consider a man who suffers from a stomach ulcer. Day after day he continues to devour hot, spicy foods which irritate the lining of the afflicted organ. All the while he claims that it is up to God to heal him, as he downs another hot pepper!

Take the asthma sufferer who continues to smoke (something not even a healthy person ought to do, if he wants to remain healthy). "O God," he prays, "help me to breathe." Meanwhile he puffs on a cigaret, adding to his distress! Or the overweight person who begs to be healed of gastritis but downs one more mouthful of spaghetti!

At times I look at my schedule and grimace, hardly believing that I have planned to keep myself *that* busy. My ministry places heavy demands on my time. Take this week, for example. I have preached and ministered in Canada every night. Several hours are spent at the typewriter each day working on this manuscript. The day after tomorrow I fly to Chicago, stay at home overnight, leave in the morning for Indianapolis to tape two television programs and arrive back in Chicago later that evening.

Most weeks follow the same pattern. Keeping this pace takes its toll, resulting in physical fatigue. In the past, I have pushed myself beyond the point of physical endurance and ended up in a sickbed. I now realize that I must *make* time for rest.

After looking at the mail, my first inclination is to accept all the invitations to preach and work myself to death. Then I realize that is exactly what I would be doing—working myself to death. Since it is difficult to preach from a hospital bed, I force myself to slow up occasionally. I have discovered that I work more effectively when my body has had proper rest, and I accomplish more for the Lord than when I neglect my physical well-being.

Epaphroditus found this out the hard way. The Apostle Paul wrote of him:

> For indeed he was sick nigh unto death: but God had mercy on him; and not on him only, but on me also, lest I should have sorrow upon sorrow. . . . Receive him therefore in the Lord with all gladness; and hold such in reputation: because for the work of Christ he was nigh unto death, not regarding his life, to supply your lack of service toward me.
>
> (Philippians 2:27, 29, 30 KJV)

The Scriptures indicate that this man was sick because he had simply overworked for the Lord, disregarding his own body in the process. ". . . But God had mercy on him . . ." (indicating that what he had done, though well-meaning, was unwise) and he was made whole again.

It's easy to joke with someone who works continually to put an extra dollar in the bank.

"You'll be the richest person in the graveyard."

For some people that is no joke—they end up a wealthy corpse, leaving all those riches to someone else.

And there is the man who has sunk so deeply into debt that he must work two or three jobs to stay ahead of the bill collector. His body is worn and tired and he can hardly stay awake in church. He drags himself through the day, one weary step after another, and wonders why he had a heart attack!

There are countless ways in which we abuse our bodies, and yet blithely expect God to make us well in spite of our actions.

The story is told of a man who would repeatedly "pray through" at the altar, only to return immediately to his old ways of living. One night, a woman overheard him pray, "O Lord, clean the cobwebs out of my heart."

Whereupon she placed her hand on his head and prayed, "Don't You do it. Lord, kill the spider."

Killing the spider solves the cobweb problem. As long as the "spider" is alive he will spin a new web. We must destroy the source of our difficulties; then fully trust the Lord to undertake for us. Isn't it presumptuous for us to continue on in our sinful or wasteful habits, assuming that God will take care of us?

A fellow-preacher once told me of an overweight woman who gorged on rich foods just before retiring to bed. All night long she moaned and groaned, rebuking the devil for making her ill. It wasn't the devil who needed to be rebuked, but the woman. She was the source of her own miseries! She had fallen into the rut of blaming the devil for everything, even when she caused her own sickness.

The Apostle Paul wrote,

> With eyes wide open to the mercies of God, I beg you my brothers, as an act of intelligent worship, to give Him your bodies as a living sacrifice, consecrated to Him and acceptable by Him.
>
> (Romans 12:1 Phillips).

Do you not know that your body is a shrine of the

65

indwelling Holy Spirit, and the Spirit is God's gift to you? You do not belong to yourselves; you were bought at a price. Then honor God in your body.

(I Corinthians 6:19,20 NEB)

Now you are together the body of Christ, and each of you is a part of it.

(I Corinthians 12:27 Phillips)

Since they belong to the Lord, our bodies are sanctified. We cannot stand before God for healing when we have not fulfilled our responsibility to keep our own bodies fit and well. We must do everything within our ability to keep our bodies healthy and strong. Maintain a balance of proper diet, work, rest and exercise. Sickness will occur less frequently. But when we do become ill, we may boldly reach out in faith and claim what is rightfully ours by inheritance. God has promised to heal us!

10

Discerning the Body of Christ

God provided ample healing for all in His Word. Yet at times healing can be most elusive, slipping easily from our grasp, escaping many altogether. Perhaps you have sought diligently for God to touch your body, without success. You may have almost given up in frustration, feeling you must be one of the exceptions. This chapter may come as a revelation to you, and it may be the door to a new life of health and strength.

The Apostle Paul discusses the abuses of Holy Communion in I Corinthians 11:27-30.

It follows that anyone who eats the bread or drinks the cup of the Lord unworthily will be guilty of desecrating the body and blood of the Lord. A man must test himself before eating his share of the bread and drinking from the cup. For he who eats and drinks eats and drinks judgment on himself if he does not discern [understand] the Body. That is why many of you are feeble and sick, and a number have died. But if we examined ourselves, we should not thus fall under judgment. When, however, we do fall under the Lord's judgment, He is disciplining us, to save us from being condemned with the rest of the world.   (NEB)

The Apostle makes it clear that this was one of the major causes of sickness *and of death*. (" . . . that is why many of you are feeble and sick, and a number have died") Their misunderstanding of the *body of Christ* was a serious charge against them.

Many Scriptures have several meanings. It is necessary to examine this portion from three perspectives.

Christ Has Taken Care of Our Sickness

Healing has been fully provided in the atonement on Calvary. Our Lord bared His back to the cruel Roman lash. It relentlessly tore His flesh and opened gaping wounds. Wounds were not the only thing opened that day! A fountain of healing and redemption became available for all people everywhere and in all times.

Isaiah caught a glimpse of the glory to come: when Messiah would pay the eternal price for our redemption. In the fourth verse of Isaiah 53 he wrote: "Surely He hath borne our griefs [disease and sicknesses] and carried our sorrows [pains] . . . He was bruised for our iniquities: the chastisement of our peace was upon Him; and with his stripes we are healed" (KJV).

68

The Apostle Peter continued this revelation in I Peter 2:24. "Who His own self bare our sins in His body on the tree, that we, being dead to sins, should live unto righteousness: by whose stripes ye were healed" (KJV). Both the Old and the New Testaments confirm that healing was brought about through those stripes so mercilessly laid upon His back.

Some would argue that these verses refer to *spiritual* healing and not to the *physical*, but this reasoning will not hold up to scriptural review. Matthew in his Gospel says: "That evening they brought Him many who were possessed by devils. He cast out the spirits with a word, and cured all who were sick. This was to fulfill the prophecy of Isaiah: 'He took our sicknesses away and carried our diseases for us' " (Matthew 8:16,17 JB). Obviously, Isaiah was referring to *physical* healing!

Let's go a step further. The Greek word, *sozoz,* denotes salvation of the soul. It is the same word used to describe healing. Its fullest meaning is "to be well, whole and physically sound," denoting total deliverance and complete safety in both soul and body. *Sozoz* is used by Jesus when He said to the leper, "Thy faith hath made thee whole" (Luke 17:19 KJV). Also, it is the word used in Luke 8:36, "He that was possessed of the devils was *healed*" (KJV).

Salvation *(sozoz)* is complete! Your full redemption was secured as each stripe was laid upon Jesus. God never planned for Christians to have sickness in their bodies or sin in their souls—the price of both has been paid. "My prayer for you, my very dear friend, is that you may be *healthy* and prosperous in every way as you are in soul" (III John 2 Phillips).

Satan no longer can lay claim upon Christians, nor can

he rightfully place upon us that which was carried by Jesus as He hung upon the cross. When we recognize Christ as our sin bearer, we no longer have to carry either our own sins or the weight of their penalties. Likewise, when we see Him as the carrier of our diseases, we no longer need be oppressed with sickness. Jesus paid it all! We cannot add to the payment by our Lord.

The penalties of sin were spiritual separation from God, sickness and disease. When Christ died on Calvary, He totally satisfied the judgments of God against every sinner who would ever be born, forever freeing us from all penalties.

Jesus was our substitute, bearing our sicknesses as well as our sins in His own body on the tree. He took our place! Isaiah says, ". . . and with His stripes we *are* healed" (Isaiah 53:5 KJV). Peter says, ". . . by whose stripes ye *were* healed" (I Peter 2:24 KJV).

No, Peter didn't use the wrong tense. Isaiah looked *forward* to the cross, but Peter looked *back* to Calvary. Isaiah used the present tense—"*are* healed,"—accepting by faith that work of redemption yet to come. The Apostle Peter points to the finished work of the cross and claims that through it "ye *were* healed." The truth of both statements is that we are *already* healed. We don't have to wait for a special occurrence to affirm the fact of our healing—it has been completed already, just as our salvation has already been finished.

Do we need some special sign from God to know we have been saved? Absolutely not! We simply accept it by faith, and believe it is done. Why then should we need some supernatural phenomenon to assure us of our healing? We are saved by believing the Word, and we receive deliverance from disease in exactly the same way.

70

An amusing incident took place one night during one of my crusades. A woman desired healing for her arthritic, inflexible back and her legs which were twisted like corkscrews. In talking with her earlier in the evening, I had prophesied that the Lord would heal her completely before the service ended. When I called her to the platform for prayer, I felt constrained by the Holy Spirit to have her read I Peter 2:24, ". . . by whose stripes ye were healed." I then explained that the work was already done, and all she had to do was accept it.

"Do you believe this?" I asked her.

"Well, I hope so," she replied.

"Read it again," I said.

"Maybe it will be tonight," was her comment.

"Not good enough!" I thought, and had her read it again and again. Suddenly, her spirit saw the truth!

"Why, I'm *already healed!*" she cried out. Instantly her back was loosed, freeing her to bend in every direction.

"Now, how about those twisted legs?" I asked. "Do you believe that God will straighten them out?"

"It surely would be nice," she commented. And so we went through the same ritual of reading and re-reading I Peter 2:24. Just as before, the light dawned and she realized the truth: that she was already healed (even though her symptoms said otherwise and her legs looked as crooked as before). Her healing was an accomplished fact of Calvary. As she accepted this by faith and began to walk falteringly toward me, her legs visibly straightened, until by the time she reached me they were normal.

Christ's Body—Not Subject to Sickness

Jesus Christ was never sick. He bore our sins, yet he was sinless. In the same manner, He bore our sicknesses, but

71

was never ill. Sin tried over and over again to attach itself to Him. "He was tempted in all points as we are, yet without sin" (Hebrews 4:15 KJV).

His life was full of extreme hardship and grueling fatigue. He walked great distances to preach the Gospel, going without sleep and fasting often. Given that sort of regimen a sick body just would not do! I'm certain that Satan attempted to kill Him with sickness on many occasions, but without success. He who triumphed over sin was master over the physical realm as well, and sickness could find no foothold in Him.

Since sin had found no place to nest, there was no curse of sin to reckon with, no sickness to combat. Jesus enjoyed perfect health. I can't imagine a sick man inspiring faith for healing in the hearts of the sick. It would be incongruous. Yet Christ inspired faith and healed thousands.

Listen carefully to what the Bible has to say about the body of Christ:

> Now you are together the body of Christ, and each of you is a part of it.
>
> (I Corinthians 12:27 Phillips)
>
> Each of us is a part of the one body of Christ . . . the Holy Spirit has fitted us all together into one body. We have been baptized into Christ's body by the one Spirit . . .
>
> (I Corinthians 12:13 TLB)
>
> Do you not know that your body is a shrine of the indwelling Holy Spirit, and the Spirit is God's gift to you? You do not belong to yourselves; you were bought at a price. Then honor God in your body.
>
> (I Corinthians 6:19,20 NEB)

What a fantastic revelation of truth! Since the Holy Spirit lives within believers, we have been incorporated into Christ's body here and now. All that He was, we (as His body) should be today. The same power and anointing that rested upon Jesus, now rests upon the Church. The same divine commission and the authority to carry it forth are now ours, for we are His body!

Christ was never touched by illness when here in the flesh, so it seems rather absurd to imagine Him manifested through the body of believers as anything but robust and healthy. I cannot visualize a sick Christ in *any* form.

If we deny the power of God to do the miraculous today, we strip Him of His deity and reduce Him to the level of an ordinary man. Many Christians believe He *used* to heal the sick, but that He doesn't anymore. Believers who listen to the enemy telling them they must be sick—that no one can expect to be well all of the time, subscribe to the same belief. Then Satan fastens some disease upon them and begins to destroy a part of the body of Christ. It should never be so! As Christ enjoyed perfect health, we also should accept nothing short of the same.

"Once the Spirit of Him who raised Christ Jesus from the dead lives within you He will, by that same Spirit, bring to your whole being, yes even your mortal bodies, new strength and vitality. For He now lives in you" (Romans 8:11 Phillips).

The Spirit of God brings absolute health, strength and well-being for spirit, soul and body; and there is no shortage of these things for those who are in Christ Jesus. You must recognize your position in the Lord and stand upon your divine prerogatives. Resist the devil. Tell him you are a part of the body of Christ and you will not allow sickness to ravage what belongs to the Lord. Rebuke him and his ailments in Jesus' name and he will flee from you, taking his sicknesses with him. Because your body belongs to the Lord, you must protect it all the more from the onslaughts of the enemy. ". . . honor God in your body" (I Corinthians 6:20 NEB).

One of the greatest healing ministries of the early 1900s was that of John G. Lake. Over a five-year period, he claimed more than 100,000 documented healings in Spokane, Washington. John Lake carried his intense beliefs over into his preaching and lifestyle. Many ridiculed him, but all respected the courage of his convictions. He taught that since Christ had already borne our sicknesses in His own body on the cross, we, as the body of Christ, need never be sick.

Lake shows the effect of the indwelling Holy Spirit on disease in the following illustration from his early ministry as a missionary in Africa.

Now watch the action of the law of life. Faith belongs to the law of life. Faith is the very opposite of fear. Faith has the opposite effect in spirit and soul and body. Faith causes the spirit of man to become confident. It causes the mind of man to become restful and positive. A positive mind repels disease. Consequently, the emanation of the Spirit destroys germs.

And because we were in contact with the Spirit of life, I and a little Dutch fellow with me went out and buried many of the people who had died from the bubonic plague. We went into the homes and carried them out, dug the graves and put them in. Sometimes we put three or four in one grave.

74

We never took the disease. Why? Because of the knowledge that the law of life in Christ Jesus protects us. That law was working. Because of the fact that a man by the action of his will, puts himself purposely in contact with God, faith takes possession of his heart, and the condition of his nature is changed. Instead of being fearful, he is full of faith. Instead of being absorbent and drawing everything to himself, his spirit repels sickness and disease. The Spirit of Christ Jesus flows through the whole being, and emanates through the hands, the heart, and from every pore of the body.

During that great plague that I mentioned, they sent a government ship with supplies and a corps of doctors. One of the doctors sent for me and said, "What have you been using to protect yourself? Our corps has this preventative and that, which we use as protection, but we concluded that if a man could stay on the ground as you have and keep ministering to the sick and burying the dead, you must have a secret. What is it?"

I answered, "Brother, that is the law of the Spirit of life in Christ Jesus. I believe that just as long as I keep my soul in contact with the living God so that His Spirit is flowing into my soul and body, that no germ will ever attach itself to me, for the Spirit of God will kill it."

He asked, "Don't you think that you had better use our preventatives?"

I replied, "No, but doctor, I think that you would like to experiment with me. If you will go over to one of these dead people and take the foam that comes out of their lungs after death, then put it under the

75

microscope you will see masses of living germs. You will find that they are alive until a reasonable time after a man is dead. You can fill my hand with them and I will keep it under the microscope, and instead of these germs remaining alive, they will die instantly."

They tried it and found it was true. They questioned, "What is that?"

I replied, "That is the law of the Spirit of life in Christ Jesus. When a man's spirit and a man's body are filled with the blessed presence of God, it oozes out of the pores of your flesh and kills the germs.

"Suppose on the other hand, my soul had been under the law of death, and I were in fear and darkness? The very opposite would have been the result. The result would have been that my body would have absorbed the germs; these would have generated disease and I would have died."*

What we believe determines, to a large extent, the state of our health. If you are persuaded that you must be sick some of the time, then some of the time you will be sick. Didn't Job confess, "The thing that I greatly feared is come upon me"? Let our minds be clear on this one point: we are the body of Christ and as such we may enjoy His strength, His vitality, His health. It belongs to us now through the "law of the spirit of life in Christ Jesus."

Many Christians say that we can glorify God when we are ill so "grin-and-bear-it." Paul asks, ". . . shall we continue in sin, that grace may abound? God forbid. How shall we, that are dead to sin, live any longer there-

---

* John G. Lake, *The John G. Lake Sermons on Dominion over Demons, Disease, and Death,* ed. Gordon Lindsay (Christ for the Nations, Inc., 1949), pp. 104,105,107,108.

in?" (Romans 6:1 KJV). Some in the church at Rome were preaching that, since grace abounded where there was much sin, it was good to sin as much as possible, for this reflected the grace of God all the more.

Today the same is true of those who preach that suffering with sickness brings glory to God. God is no more glorified by your sickness than He is by your sin. The best way to glorify or honor God is with a healthy body which reflects His handiwork. Any praise God receives from our suffering is in spite of the sickness, *not* because of it!

We honor Him when our bodies are well and strong, proving that the Word of God is true and that healing is for today. When we are healed it strips away all doubts as to the veracity of God; but when we patiently endure our ailments, we cast aspersions upon the truth of His Word.

Disunity in the Body

We have seen that we are the body of Christ as it now exists in flesh and blood. The body of Christ is made up of all believers, regardless of their denominational affiliations. If a person has taken Christ as Lord and Savior, that automatically makes him part of Christ's body. All believers are equal heirs to the promises of God. Our faith, and nothing else, brings us into this relationship! Through Christ's death on Calvary, we are intricately linked together in a spiritual network, just as the nerves, sinews, tendons and muscles together make up a human body.

And so become more and more in every way like Christ who is the head of His body, the Church. Under His direction the whole body is fitted together perfectly, and each part in its own special way helps the other parts, so that the whole body is

77

healthy and growing and full of love.

(Ephesians 4:15,16 TLB)

As the human body, which has many parts, is a unity, and those parts, despite their multiplicity, constitute one single body, so it is with Christ. For we are all baptized by the one Spirit into one body. . . . Now the body is not one part, but many. If the foot should say, "Because I am not a hand I don't belong to the body," does that alter the fact that the foot is a part of the body? Or if the ear should say, "Because I am not an eye I don't belong to the body," does that mean that the ear really is no part of the body? . . . The fact is there are many parts but only one body. So that the eye cannot say to the hand, "I don't need you!" nor, again, can the head say to the feet, "I don't need you!" . . . But God has harmonized the whole body by giving importance of function to the parts which lack apparent importance, that the body should work together as a whole with all the members in sympathetic relationship with one another. So it happens that if *one* member suffers *all* the other members suffer with it, and if *one* member is honored *all* the members share a common joy. Now you are together the body of Christ, and each of you is a part of it.

(I Corinthians 12:12-27 Phillips)

The church at Corinth, to whom Paul was addressing his remarks, was certainly not without its problems, a major one of which was their many divisions:

. . . When ye come together in the church, I hear that there be divisions among you.

(I Corinthians 11:18 KJV)

Now I beg of you, my brothers, by all that the

Lord Jesus Christ means to you, to speak with one voice, and not allow yourselves to be split up into parties . . . You are each making different claims—"I am one of Paul's men," says one; "I am one of Apollos'," says another; or "I am one of Cephas';" while someone else says, "I owe my faith to Christ alone." What are you saying? Is there more than one Christ?

(I Corinthians 1:10-12 Phillips)

One of the greatest deterrents to the free flowing of the Holy Spirit in many of our churches is division among the brethren: brother against brother, sister against sister, church members fighting the pastor, and the pastor warring against the people. Bitterness runs like a river from one person to another. Hard feelings become high barriers between groups. Hatred eats like a cancer at the inner parts of the church. Unpleasant happenings of long ago loom like haunting spectors, never dying.

"I'll *never* forget what he did to me!" someone says belligerently.

Someone else replies, "And I'll get even, if it takes me *forever!*"

How it must grieve the heart of God to see His children so divided!

We see this insidious working of the enemy even among the clergy, as they fight each other in the name of Christianity. Often there is open antagonism toward other churches. I am not referring here to heretical sects that are anti-Christian, but to those who are of fundamentally the same faith. And this situation is far too common.

Bitterness, strife, anger, selfishness, malice, competition, hard feelings, jealousy, resentments—*all* take their toll upon the one manifesting them!

79

Saul of Tarsus journeyed on the road to Damascus with legal documents granting him permission to persecute the believers there. Suddenly he was stricken to the ground by a blinding light. "And he fell to the earth, and he heard a voice saying unto him, Saul, Saul, why persecutest thou me? And he said, Who art thou Lord? And the Lord said, I am Jesus whom thou persecutest" (Acts 9:4,5 KJV).

How could Saul have been persecuting Jesus when this event transpired many years after the ascension? Christ was not present in physical form on the earth. Was the Lord mistaken when He said, "I am Jesus whom thou persecutest?" God makes no mistakes. He *is* present: in the form of His Church, in the heart of every believer regardless of how insignificant that one may seem.

Saul was "breathing out threatenings and slaughter against the disciples of the Lord" (Acts 9:1 KJV), and in so doing, was putting his hands on Christ Himself!

"And I, the King, will tell them, 'When you did it to these my brothers *you were doing it to me*' " (Matthew 25:40 TLB). When you touch one of the brethren, for good or ill, you have touched Christ Himself. It is not a casual thing to hold grudges and ill-feelings toward a brother or sister in the Lord. Those cutting words that were hurled at a Christian sliced deeply into the heart of God Himself.

When Saul put his hands on the disciples to persecute them, he was committing a gross sin and was stricken blind by God for it! Like Saul, many Christians are also smitten of God—for they have touched His Body to do it harm. You cannot hurt God's body, and expect that your body will not feel the effect of it.

Continued health and well-being in the physical body cannot be maintained without a harmony of functions

80

among the many organs and members. In the same way, long-lasting vitality withers when division and discord exist among the members of Christ. There are many sound physical reasons why this is so, apart from the spiritual law of "sowing and reaping." Our bodies produce various kinds of poisonous substances from anger, jealousy, resentment and fear. If continued over a period of time, they will cause many physical ailments.

It was for this cause, "not understanding the body of Christ," that many were sick in the church at Corinth and several had died. Apart from the physical side effects of wrong attitudes (which are produced automatically, whether directed at Christians or sinners), we must also reckon with God. He does not tolerate Christians destroying Christians. It is a serious thing to fight against another believer for by that action, one may bring about his own downfall. ". . . Touch not mine anointed, and do my prophets no harm" (I Chronicles 16:22 KJV). God's exhortation has never changed down through the years.

The following Scriptures point out the seriousness of right attitudes.

God will rightly repay with injury those who are injuring you. (II Thessalonians 1:6 JB)

In this way we distinguish the children of God from the children of the devil: anybody . . . not loving his brother is no child of God's. This is the message as you heard it from the beginning: that we are to love one another; not to be like Cain, who belonged to the Evil One and cut his brother's throat. . . . If you refuse to love, you must remain dead: to hate your brother is to be a murderer, and murderers, as you know, do not have eternal life in them.

(I John 3:10-12,15 JB)

81

But if a man says, "I love God," while hating his brother, he is a liar. If he does not love the brother whom he has seen, it cannot be that he loves God whom he has not seen. And indeed this command comes to us from Christ himself; that he who loves God must also love his brother.

(I John 4:20,21 NEB)

These and many other verses clearly indicate the heavy priority God places upon having and manifesting true love for one another.

James 2:13 tells us: "The man who makes no allowances for others will find none made for him" (Phillips).

George Herbert is quoted as having said, "He who cannot forgive destroys the bridge over which he himself must pass." Read prayerfully Matthew 18:21-35. In this portion, Peter asks Jesus how many times he should forgive someone who wrongs him—would seven times be enough? The Lord replies that seventy times seven (490 times) would be more correct. Then he went on to illustrate His point with a story.

A king called all his debtors before him to pay their bills. One man owed the king 7,500,000 ounces of gold (10,000 talents). When he admitted that he could not pay off his indebtedness, the king demanded that the man and his whole household should be sold. The debtor begged and pleaded for his life until the king showed him mercy. The entire obligation (amounting to several millions of dollars in today's currency) was pardoned.

Immediately afterwards, the man went out and found a fellow servant who owed him twelve and a half ounces of gold (only a few dollars) and threw him into prison for being unable to pay the debt! When the king heard what this unforgiving servant had done, he had him thrown into prison and turned over to the tormentors.

Jesus completes this story with this statement: "And that is how my heavenly Father will deal with you unless you each forgive your brother from your heart" (vs.35 JB).

"And when you stand praying, if you have a grievance against anyone, forgive him, so that your Father in heaven may forgive you the wrongs you have done" (Mark 11:25 NEB). The Scriptures teach that our forgiveness is predicated upon our willingness to forgive others. If this premise is correct, then multiplied sins have accumulated upon millions of Christians. These sins remain unforgiven by God. The accounts are yet standing, even though they have earnestly and sincerely prayed and asked for forgiveness. They have not complied with God's law of sowing and reaping: forgiving in order to be forgiven.

In the Lord's Prayer we are instructed to pray, "Forgive us our trespasses *as we forgive* those who trespass against us." The words "as we forgive" mean *in the same way*. To put it simply, "Forgive me in the same way that I have forgiven my neighbor."

How is your account? Have you taken inventory while reading this chapter? If you refuse to extend forgiveness to *anyone* then for an equal period of time, *your sins have gone unforgiven by God!* Some soul-searching may be called for but the results can prove rewarding, and ultimately lead to your healing.

Someone may say he has no grievance with a brother, but the brother has something against him. Is he liable for someone else's actions or thoughts? What does the Bible have to say about this?

> If when you are bringing your gift to the altar [an act of worship], you suddenly remember that your brother has a grievance against you, leave your gift where it is before the altar [don't proceed any further with your worship]. First go and make your peace with your brother, and only then come back and offer your gift.   (Matthew 5:23,24 NEB)

God considers your relationship with your brother of greater consequence than your worship of Him. Does that statement shock you? It shouldn't, because your relationship with God is seriously diminished when your relationship with His Son (the body of Christ) is adversely affected. God recognizes that there are some people who will not allow you to reconcile the "bad blood" between you no matter how sincerely you approach them in the love of Christ. But that does not absolve you of the responsibility to go to them and attempt to make peace. "If possible, so far as it depends upon you, live peaceably with all men" (Romans 12:18 RSV).

We read in the book of James, "So confess your sins to one another, and pray for one another, and this will cure you" (James 5:16 JB). The Phillips translation says: "You should get into the habit of admitting your sins to each other . . . so that you may be healed."

In the past, some have misunderstood that Scripture, and have admitted publicly all kinds of foolish sins, only to find out that it has seriously curtailed their effectiveness for the Lord. This is not what James had in mind. The context makes it obvious that he means for brothers and sisters who have wronged each other to "clear the air" between them, so their prayers will not be hindered.

Calling for the elders of the church to anoint one with

oil has often been an empty ritual because one refuses to follow the further injunction of James to "confess your sins" (if needed). God is the healer, and if we are to be healed, we will have to approach Him on His terms. This includes the responsibility for making peace if we have wronged a brother or sister. That is our sowing. The reaping will be a strong, healthy body with which to glorify the Lord.

What does the Bible have to say about loving one another? "Love your neighbor as yourself. Love cannot wrong a neighbor; therefore the whole law is summed up in love" (Romans 13:9,10 NEB).

If one is truly filled with the love of Christ, he will automatically love the brethren. "For no man ever yet hated his own flesh" (Ephesians 5:29 KJV). Perhaps you feel as though you *can't* love that person—some people *are* quite unlovable. Just to be around them makes you uneasy. Your personalities clash.

Perhaps this incident will help you to discover the way of love for the unlovable. A minister severely attacked my ministry. He openly declared from the pulpit that everything I had preached was "garbage" and attempted to prevent me from ministering in another church in his community by lying about my ministry and character.

My first inclination was to bring him before his superiors to be reprimanded and censured. I made out a long list of charges against him. Then I prayed that the Lord would bless my efforts and help me in my struggle to rectify this gross injustice to my ministry.

God spoke to me and acknowledged that I had the scriptural right to demand that his superiors censure him. According to the bylaws of his organization, it was also proper to do so. But that wasn't what He wanted me to do.

85

God said to me, "I want you to *love* him!"

"I can't do that!" I cried. "It just isn't in me to love him—he's hurt me so!"

The Holy Spirit gently replied, "I *know* it isn't within you to love him, so allow Me to love him through you."

What an eye-opener that was for me! The love I could not manufacture, God could implant within me—it would be God's love, not mine! He would love him through my broken heart, if I permitted Him. How I wept before the Lord as wave after wave of divine love swept over my spirit.

Then the Spirit of God continued to speak to my heart. True, God would show the minister His love through me, but if he refused to repent then God would judge him.

The Spirit continued, "Since he has publicly held your ministry up to ridicule, my hand will rest heavily in judgment upon him. Until he has you stand in his pulpit and publicly reconciles himself to you, admitting before the people that he has sinned against my servant, he will feel the weight of my punishment."

This rang chillingly true in my heart, for at the very moment I had received the news of his vilification of my ministry, God had prepared a prophecy for me in the heart of a woman praying at the altar. She arose and came to the last pew where I was sitting (knowing absolutely nothing of the news I had just received), and quietly asked me, "May I prophesy to you?" When I answered in the affirmative, she continued, "The Lord knows the persecution that you are going through. He sees that one who is attacking you. The Lord will sustain and uphold you, and you will stand like a wall of brass. God will judge that one for you, and bring you through victorious!"

Had she prophesied that to me five minutes earlier, I

would not have known what she was referring to, but God's timing is always perfect!

The morning following that incident I received a phone call. The caller knew nothing of the previous night's prophecy but the Spirit of God had repeatedly impressed on her that morning to call me with certain verses. Although she was ignorant of their meaning for me, He had assured her that I would fully understand. Each Scripture that she relayed to me told how God would avenge me of my adversary, and that I was not to take judgment into my own hands. You can see how I nearly missed the mind of the Spirit by preparing to bring this man before his presbytery.

One day I suggested that a friend join me for lunch. Afterwards we strolled through a shopping plaza which had over seventy stores.

I have never been a sports-minded person—sports simply don't interest me. So when I suggested that we enter a sporting goods store to browse, I couldn't understand it myself. I simply *felt* that was where I should go. Out of seventy stores, in the one I was *least* likely to enter, there stood the minister who had wronged me. Without a doubt, God had arranged our rendezvous.

I approached him in a spirit of love and quietly told him I had been informed of his statements. I explained that my first reaction was to bring him before his superiors on charges of ministerial misconduct.

Even his eyes and tone of voice betrayed his bitterness as he spoke. "Go ahead and do what you very well please," he answered. "See if I care!"

Humanly, it would have been almost impossible to have loved him at that moment—he was so unlovable. But my heart overflowed with great love and deep pity toward him. With tears in my eyes I told him that it was no longer my intention to take up charges against him.

"The Holy Spirit has filled my heart with love for you," I said. "I'll always be there if you ever need me."

It wasn't easy to tell him the rest, but I had to or else answer to God for *my* disobedience. I repeated the words God had spoken through three distinct sources: the women who had come to me and the direct voice of the Spirit in my heart. What the minister had done, he would have to undo in the same manner—publicly. God would judge him until he complied.

Without a word of apology or comment, the minister and his wife walked away. Throughout our conversation his wife had remained silent. Watching her go, I knew by the Spirit that she would shortly lose the baby they had wanted so desperately. (She showed no sign of pregnancy. They had confided to me at one time that it seemed impossible for her to conceive. I don't know whether or not *she* knew at that moment that she was carrying a child.)

I told this to my wife and my mother so that when it happened there would be no doubt that it was part of God's judgment. Within the next several months it happened exactly as I had said. I went to God in prayer on their behalf and asked that He now lift His judgment and bless them.

The Spirit of God said, "You continue to love him, and I will continue to judge him. I have given him the conditions under which I will lift my wrath. Let him meet My demands. There is no other way."

Since that time I have written him on several occasions and each letter has been unanswered. Following his wife's miscarriage he was taken seriously ill and remained so for most of the year. Not only has he felt the pressure physically, but spiritually as well. Recently he confessed from his pulpit that for a year and a half (covering the period since he attacked my ministry) he had been completely backslidden and away from God. Yet, the words the Holy Spirit demanded never came. The last I heard was that his body was still very weak.

Every time I pray for him asking for God's judgment to lift, the answer is always the same: "Let Me tend to that. You just pray for him; I'll do the rest." Inwardly I know there is no way he can escape what he has brought upon himself. Only *he* has the key to unlock God's forgiveness. It is a serious thing to have touched the Body of Christ. "Touch not mine anointed, and do my prophets no harm" (I Chronicles 16:22 KJV) is still the Word of God today.

If we could only view our actions, words and deeds against our fellow believers through the eyes of God, and have a clear picture of the waiting consequences, we would act so differently toward each other. We would *love* so much more!

The love that a man cannot produce, God will generate through a heart yielded to Him, for love is a fruit of the Spirit. Jesus never said men would be convinced that we are true disciples by our spiritual gifts, or the mighty power that we manifest, or the lofty testimonies that we give. He simply said, "Now I am giving you a new command—love one another. Just as I have loved you, so you must love one another. This is how all men will know that you are my disciples, because you have such love for one another" (John 13:34,35 Phillips).

11

Why Ask More than Once?

"If at first you don't succeed, try, try again!" One of the most difficult lessons one must learn in life (and some never do) is that we don't get everything we want the first time we ask for it.

Name anyone who is a success in his field. Usually that person has learned to "stick with it" through good times and bad, highs and lows. We see the end results—success and prestige—unaware of the many hard times he previously endured in secret.

In a television interview recently, a famous person mentioned how he "starved" for three years before his "break" came and the public began to take notice of him. Anything worth having is worth waiting for.

This is certainly true in the realm of divine healing. However, there are great numbers of people who have missed their blessing because of a lack of perseverance. We must approach the subject of healing with a resolution and steadfastness that will not diminish until the blessing *promised* is a blessing *realized*.

It is so much easier to give up than to be relentless. That is probably why there are more followers than leaders; more failures than success stories. The Gospels have taught me that the life of Jesus was the perfect illustration of singleness of purpose.

Perhaps you have been prayed for several times and you haven't seen any outward manifestation of your healing, so you've decided to "pick up your marbles, and go home." You're going to quit and resign yourself to being ill.

"The Lord knows where I live," you say, "and when He's good and ready, He can come and heal me. I'm tired of praying and getting nowhere."

We get in such a rush when we want God to do something for us! If we've prayed once or twice and didn't get an immediate answer, then that's the last of it. But look at any of the heroes of faith. Can you discover *one* who wasn't a man or woman of persistent faith? Real faith will not let go, but takes hold of the promises of God with a bulldog tenacity until they come to pass.

Jesus had just raised a girl from the dead, we read in Matthew 9:27-30 (Phillips).

"As Jesus passed on His way two blind men followed Him with the cry, 'Have pity on us, Son of David!' And when He had gone inside the house these two came up to Him."

They had been pursuing him some distance through the

city streets, asking to be healed. When He reached the house where He was staying, they simply followed Him in and *kept on asking* until they got what they were after.

"Then He touched their eyes, saying, 'You have believed and so it shall be.' And their sight returned."

What a picture that makes! Two blind men being jostled about in the large crowds that always surrounded the Lord—pushed away by the unconcerned, yet undaunted in their efforts to be healed. By their perseverance they made recorded history. Had they stopped short of their goal, they would have died obscure, blind beggars.

Next, let us consider the story of the Syrophoenician woman whose daughter was tormented by a demon. She learned that Jesus was passing through her community. Having heard of His power, she had hope for her daughter where there had been no hope before. But the question was: how was she to get to Him? The crowds milling around Him were large. She reached the edge of the throng surrounding Him, ". . . and started shouting, 'Sir, Son of David, take pity on me. My daughter is tormented by a devil' " (Matthew 15:22b JB). Surely Jesus Christ wouldn't turn away from her desperate cry. But the Scripture says, ". . . He answered her not a word" (v. 23).

Many might have turned away at this point and thought: *That man thinks he's better than everyone else. Won't even talk to me. Well, so what? I really didn't want to talk with Him anyhow!*

But that wasn't this woman's attitude. "And His disciples went and pleaded with Him. 'Give her what she wants,' they said, 'because she is shouting after us' " (v. 23b). She refused to be ignored; her voice could be heard above the crowd. Only Jesus could meet her need and she

92

knew it. When she finally got her interview with the Lord He pointed out that she was a Gentile.

"It is not fair to take the children's food and throw it to the house dogs" (a common Jewish idiom, meaning Gentiles) (v.26).

Surely she would leave now—but she didn't. "She retorted, 'Ah yes, sir; but even house dogs can eat the scraps that fall from their master's table.' Then Jesus answered her, 'Woman, you have great faith. Let your wish be granted.' And from that moment her daughter was well again" (vs. 27,28).

Her resolution to get what she came after is a perfect illustration of the diligence of real faith. The kind of faith that obtains results. The Word of God shows that genuine faith doesn't quit when the going gets rough; rather faith *thrives* on tests!

Mark writes about blind Bartimaeus, a beggar in the city of Jericho. "When Bartimaeus heard that Jesus from Nazareth was near, he began to shout out, 'Jesus, Son of David, have mercy on me!' 'Shut up!' some of the people yelled at him. But he only shouted the louder, again, and again, 'O Son of David, have mercy on me!' " (Mark 10: 47,48 TLB).

Let the crowd yell at Bartimaeus and tell him to be quiet. It didn't deter him at all. But if he was to be heard at all he had to shout louder. So he did— again and again. When he got his audience with the Lord, he also received his eyesight!

Was it worth all the embarrassment, harassment and effort? When you get to heaven, ask Bartimaeus. If you can't wait, ask any one of the thousands of present-day believers who have received their healing by persistently pressing through to the Master.

Ask, for instance, the young lady tormented with multiple sclerosis who came to one of our services in Chicago. Fifty doctors hadn't freed her from her physical problems. She seriously contemplated suicide as the only solution to her painful existence. After attending many healing services she still was not well.

When I returned to Chicago some months later, she attended the services again, anxiously awaiting God's healing. But it was several more nights before the pain was totally relieved. Persistent faith brought its reward as waves of the Holy Spirit swept over her.

Jesus told the crowds a parable about the need to pray continually and without wavering.

"There was a judge in a certain town," He said, "who had neither fear of God nor respect for man. In the same town there was a widow who kept on coming to him and saying, 'I want justice from you against my enemy!' For a long time he refused, but at last he said to himself, 'Maybe I have neither fear of God nor respect for man, but since she keeps pestering me I must give this widow her just rights, or she will persist in coming and worry me to death.' "

And the Lord said, "You notice what the unjust judge has to say? Now will not God see justice done to His chosen who cry to Him day and night even when He delays to help them? I promise you, He will see justice done to them, and done speedily."

(Luke 18:1-7 JB)

My business manager, Arthur Warner, told me a story that took place when he was serving in the same capacity with another evangelist. Their tent stood on the outskirts of a large city in Alabama for a ten-day revival. The meetings were charged with the power of God. Many healings took place nightly as the evangelist prayed and laid hands on the sick.

At the first meeting one little boy, carried in his father's arms, captured Art's attention. The boy was totally blind. The doctors confirmed that he would never see again—there was nothing medical science could do for him.

The evangelist laid hands on the boy's head and prayed with sincerity and fervor. After prayer he removed his hands from the child's eyes and asked, "Can you see?"

Hearts sank as the little lad said, "No," and his father took him away.

But who do you suppose appeared in the prayer line the very next night? That father and his little boy! They were not going to let one temporary setback discourage their faith. Prayer was offered for him again.

Nothing happened.

Every night Art saw the father standing in the prayer line with his little boy in his arms. Every night Art watched him walk away with no results. *Nine times* they came and went.

On the tenth and final night of the revival they took their place in the prayer line for the last time. Outwardly there was nothing different about the order and anointing of God on the service that night. But this meeting *was* different for one little blind boy. Now he could see!

What might have happened had that father given up in discouragement after the first few nights of failure? That blind boy would now be a blind man, locked in a prison of darkness.

Since all earlier attempts to obtain healing had failed, I am convinced that his persistence alone brought the desired results. Like the woman in the Gospel of Luke who kept coming to the judge, this father got what he came after. He would not be denied. His adversary was forced to bow before him and his son's blindness had to flee!

Who is this adversary? He is the enemy of our spirit, soul and body—Satan. He will do his utmost to afflict us. He drains our vital energies which could be used to build God's Kingdom. He steals the joy of living from every one of God's children through sickness and weakness. Have you ever prayed and prayed, but the answer seemed even farther away from becoming a reality than before? The heavens seemed to be made of brass as your pain grew worse and harder to bear? Hope and faith seemed to be mere words?

In times like that, remember the scriptural examples we've discussed and just keep on praying until light breaks through! The promises of God are not only for those who *ask,* but for those who will go beyond that first step and fervently and earnestly seek the face of God for their healing. Those who will knock again and again (like the widow with the unjust judge) will see their desire become a reality. If in this Christian life you learn anything, let it be perseverance in prayer, and all the blessings of our heavenly Father will find their way to your door.

12

Money and Healing

Even from the days of your fathers ye are gone away from mine ordinances, and have not kept them. Return unto me, and I will return unto you, saith the Lord of hosts. But ye said, Wherein shall we return?

Will a man rob God? Yet ye have robbed me. But ye say, Wherein have we robbed thee? In tithes and offerings.

Ye are cursed with a curse: for ye have robbed Me, even this whole nation.

Bring ye all the tithes into the storehouse, that there may be meat in mine house, and prove me now herewith, saith the Lord of hosts, if I will not open

you the windows of heaven, and pour you out a
blessing, that there shall not be room enough to receive it.

And I will rebuke the devourer for your sakes . . ..
(Malachi 3:7-11a KJV)

The Christian's obligations to use finances properly for
the upbuilding of the kingdom of God are outlined in the
Scriptures. God holds every individual responsible for all
that is entrusted to him. The Bible refers to us as *stewards,*
or agents, in charge of His wealth. We must realize that all
we have really belongs to God. We are responsible for the
astute management of His property.

"But it shall come to pass, if thou wilt not hearken unto
the voice of the Lord thy God, to observe to do all His
commandments and His statutes [laws] which I command
thee this day; that all these curses shall come upon thee
and overtake thee . . .." (Deuteronomy 28:15 KJV).

Immediately following this verse of Scripture, the Lord
spells out a long list of sicknesses, plagues and judgments
which would befall the children of Israel if they disobeyed
His laws. But God addressed those who would be
obedient, also. "If thou wilt diligently hearken to the voice
of the Lord thy God, and wilt do that which is right in His
sight, and wilt give ear to His commandments, and keep
all His statutes, I will put none of these diseases upon thee,
which I have brought upon the Egyptians: for I am the
Lord that healeth thee" (Exodus 15:26 KJV).

God's desire is to heal all His children, but He has rules
by which He operates. We cannot violate them and expect
Him to overlook it. He has stated that our health depends
upon keeping His commandments. Disobedience brings
sickness upon the children of God.

Let's begin here with the realm of finances. At least ten

percent (a tithe) of everything we earn belongs to God. In Malachi 3, God accused Israel of robbing Him. When they asked how, God replied, "In tithes and offerings."

Jesus Christ often gave financial advice which renewed the emphasis God had placed upon giving. The Word is clear: if we don't keep God's commandments, we cannot expect His blessings; rather, we can look for His judgment.

Consider the weight of God's statement that any man who holds back that which He requires has actually stolen from God. Many Christians do that. Week after week they never give God a thought when the paycheck is brought home. They spend the money as though they owned it all.

Tithing as a scriptural principle sets the point at which to *begin* giving. Why limit giving to a meager ten percent with all that God has done for us? "For God so loved . . . that He gave . . ." (John 3:16 KJV). Love can often be measured by the freedom with which an individual gives to God. (But it cannot be measured by the *amount* of the gift—to people of modest means, giving "freely" still constitutes a relatively "small" *amount*. However, God may see their pittance as a great gift out of their meager stores. Perhaps God gauges the liberality of our giving not so much by what we give, as by how much we have left for ourselves *after* giving!)

In one of my pastorates I had a deacon who refused to tithe. "Tithing was only under the old dispensation," he argued. "That's not for today! We're under grace, not under the law."

A close look at the Bible shows that tithing was established *before* the law was ever instituted, and confirmed again by Jesus Christ: ". . . For you tithe down to the last mint leaf in your garden . . . *yes, you should tithe* . . ." (Matthew 23:23 TLB). Tithing is not the standard of giving; it is simply a *foundation* upon which our giving is structured.

One Sunday I visited the deacon's house. *He* brought up the subject of tithing, as he often did. I think he was attempting to convince himself that he was justified in withholding from the Lord what was rightfully His. He would always get red-faced and angry when he talked about giving.

I said to him, "It is my conviction that if we don't tithe, God may exact the money from us through some calamity, perhaps a sickness, an accident or by some other means. We really are on shaky ground when we steal from God. That's what Malachi says we are doing when we refuse to give God at least ten percent—for that already belongs to Him."

He laughingly brushed aside my warning. Before I left he showed me the new room they had just added to the back of the house. It was beautiful—but I couldn't help thinking, *As beautiful as this room is, it was built with God's money.*

Their house was nestled at the base of lush, rolling hills in the country. Just a few days later, a neighboring farmer left his tractor unattended at the top of a hill directly behind the deacon's house. He thought the brake was on—but it wasn't! That tractor demolished the brand-new room. Under normal circumstances, insurance funds would have covered the rebuilding costs. Not so in this instance. There were legal technicalities involved so that the bill had to be paid out of the deacon's own pocket. Coincidence?

Soon afterward this same deacon was admitted into the

hospital with a serious back condition which has lasted ever since. He returned to the hospital at least twice during the months that I remained as pastor. Before our discussions about robbing from God he had boasted of never being sick. Afterwards, he became chronically ill.

Coincidence again? If God is robbed, He will not take it lightly. He may exact His own—possibly with interest. Wasn't it God Himself who said that for this cause (withholding tithes and offerings) "Ye are cursed with a curse; for ye have robbed Me . . ."?

A leading preacher once said he would pray with a man who didn't tithe, but he wouldn't close his eyes. He figured that any man who would rob from God wouldn't hesitate to rob from him also!

One of the danger zones of our day is in credit spending. Many of us own several credit cards, which we use quite regularly. When we want something, we simply say "charge it." It's so easy to have anything the heart desires: credit brings it within reach of practically everyone.

Economists tell us that the American public is in debt for the next ten years, excluding house mortgages. If mortgages are included, the figure becomes a staggering 25 years! We owe for cars, washing machines, furniture, boats, toys, color TV's, stereos, summer cottages, exotic vacations, and the list goes on and on.

For example, there's a woman who charges a great amount of Christmas toys for her children. Then she works until the following November to pay off the debt, but starts to charge all over again for another Christmas! Often this is the kind of person who "can't afford to tithe."

When Christians go overboard in debt, they are unable to give God His portion. This means that we rob God for the sake of our own pleasures, giving His money to the bank or credit card company as though it were our own.

"Have you forgotten that the Kingdom of God will never belong to the wicked . . . or the thief?" (I Corinthians 6:10 Phillips). If God will not place His blessings upon someone who has stolen from another *man,* will He heal someone who steals from the storehouse of heaven?

When we withhold our tithes and offerings, we steal from God. It is rather ludicrous to hold back from God with one hand and have the other hand extended to Him for healing.

Pledges compose another part of Christian stewardship. A pledge is a promise made to the Lord. Frequently, Christians feel moved upon by the Holy Spirit to make a financial commitment to some worthy cause of the Gospel, and pledge themselves accordingly. As time goes by, they sometimes lose the original zeal that prompted this obligation, and feel as though it is unimportant to fulfill such a promise. After all, who will know if they don't?

> . . . This is the thing which the Lord commanded. If a man vow a vow unto the Lord . . . he shall not break his word, he shall do according to all that proceedeth out of his mouth.
>
> (Numbers 30:1b,2 KJV)

> Offer unto God thanksgiving; and pay thy vows unto the most High: and call upon Me in the day of trouble: I will deliver thee . . .
>
> (Psalm 50:14,15 KJV)

You see, God has enjoined the Christian to pay his vows and *then* to call upon Him, and He will bring deliverance. You may feel the way some people do who say, "Yes, I made that financial pledge to the work of

102

God, but afterwards I changed my mind."

"When thou vowest a vow unto God, defer not to pay it; for He hath no pleasure in fools: pay that which thou hast vowed. Better is it that thou shouldest not vow, than that thou shouldest vow and not pay" (Ecclesiastes 5:4,5 KJV). God said when you have made your commitment, don't put off paying it, for it will be required of you just the same.

By civil law, signing your name to a contract binds you to perform it. A contract is not an easy thing to break. Making an agreement with the Lord for a specified amount is of even greater importance. Through Malachi God said that the only way for Israel to have the curses lifted from them was to repent, and pay their vows—to give their tithes and offerings to the Lord. Then He said He would rebuke the devourer for their sakes, and He would *heal* their land.

Take time to examine yourself. Have you been guilty of financial negligence? If so, make up your mind to fulfill your obligations to the Lord, and "pay your vows." When you have done your part, then you may reach out in faith and believe that the Lord will hear you and "rebuke the devourer" for your sake.

13

Asking with Confidence

". . . We can approach God with confidence, and obtain from Him whatever we ask, because we are keeping His commands and doing what He approves" (I John 3:22 NEB).

Here is the key that opens the door of God's vast storehouse where all His manifold blessings wait to be discovered. It is quite simple: *obedience*. Nothing more.

A parallel can be found in the natural realm. We educate our children to understand that if they are to reap the extras of life, they must obey their parents. To disobey means to forfeit some prize. Children soon learn that everything in life is not free, that there is a price to be paid for enjoying some things. My own children have learned from experience that if they want something, they must obey the rules of the household. If they break these rules, we withhold some of their privileges.

The Scriptures reveal God as our heavenly Father, who also has certain rules and regulations for the divine household. The Word of God reveals that God has attached certain of His benefits to His unbreakable laws. Healing is one such favor.

The verse quoted at the beginning of this chapter makes it evident that answers to prayer are contingent upon keeping God's commands. Can you recall the time when you were a child and knew you had done something wrong? If Dad was aware of it, you couldn't approach him boldly for anything. You were certain that what you really deserved was to be punished. Your normal confidence in asking for something was gone.

It is no different when sin comes between the Christian and his heavenly Father—it weakens our confidence. Disobedience to His commands impedes Christian growth and prevents us from receiving God's promises.

When God had led the children of Israel out of Egypt's bondage, it was His desire that they live blamelessly before Him, and that He would be their complete source of supply for spirit, soul and body. After all, there was nothing they could need or want that could not be found in Him.

His vast power unfolded before them as they were led of the Spirit through the wilderness. He provided their food by sending manna down from heaven each night; their clothes and sandals never wore out; and they saw water pour from the rock to quench their thirst. He had healed all who left Egypt and there was not a sick person among their tribes. *But would God heal every disease?*

The Lord stripped away any doubts that mankind would ever have concerning His ability and His desire to heal. ". . . There He made for them a statute [law] and an ordinance . . . and said, If thou wilt diligently hearken to the voice of the Lord thy God, and wilt do that which is right in His sight, and wilt give ear to His commandments, and keep all His statutes, I will put none of these diseases upon thee, which I have brought upon the Egyptians: for I am the Lord that healeth thee" (Exodus 15:26 KJV). In the Hebrew the term used in this verse to describe God is *Jehovah (Yahweh) Raphah,* literally interpreted "the Lord that *heals.*"

Here we have a revelation of the nature of God—He has disclosed that it is His nature to heal! We have already discussed the unchanging nature of God the Father ("For I am the Lord, I change not . . ." Malachi 3:6 KJV), and also of Christ ("Jesus Christ the same yesterday, and today, and forever." Hebrews 13:8 KJV). God has clearly disclosed His nature and His nature *never* varies from one day to the next.

Having established the fact that He was a God who wanted to heal His people, He then laid down certain ground rules. The children of Israel were enjoined to keep the statutes of God if they wanted to share in His favor. Of course the opposite was also true: breaking God's commandments would incur His wrath. They would be sick, like the Egyptians who refused to listen to God speaking through His servant Moses.

The world today is cultivating a spirit of independence. We can see it in the many new organizations which seek to establish the self-direction and autonomy of man. This spirit of "I'll do it my way" has carried over into the hearts of many church people, and has been the cause of much damage to their spiritual lives.

There are lessons to be learned from Israel's experiences with God: 1) that it pays to obey the Lord and 2) there are consequences to be paid for wilfulness. Whenever the Israelites obeyed the Lord, they enjoyed fullest blessings. When "every man did that which was right in his own eyes" (Judges 17:6 KJV), the nation felt the heavy wrath of God. God has placed disobedience (rebellion) on the same low level as witchcraft! (See I Samuel 15:23 KJV.)

In August of 1957 our evangelistic party drove into the little town of Thule Lake, California. The temperature was high and so were our expectations, for we believed that the Holy Spirit had directed us to that town and would grant us a great revival there. All three of us on the team were tense, like horses at the starting gate, anxious for what we believed would be a tremendous move of the Holy Spirit in that community.

The first service finally arrived. As the singing progressed, I sensed that something was wrong in that church. The service couldn't have posed more difficulties if it had had a mind of its own. Strong forces were at work under the surface to undermine the work of the Holy Spirit. But what was wrong? Who was responsible?

Many questions raced through my mind as I delivered the sermon of the evening. I ended early. The words which normally would have flowed were impossible to summon. The strain was intense.

The next few nights the situation remained the same. One evening in desperation I stopped preaching, bowed my head and prayed a simple prayer. I asked the Holy Spirit to reveal to me the problem. In that brief moment, God told me that a married man seated toward the rear of the church was having an affair. As a result, God's judgment had fallen upon the congregation.

Desperately seeking God's wisdom, I asked the audience to bow their heads so not to embarrass the guilty party. I revealed what the Holy Spirit had showed me, saying simply that it was someone in the congregation. He was the only person who refused to bow his head.

I said, "This man knows exactly to whom I'm referring, because he is looking right at me now." I then proceeded to give him an invitation to repent of his sin and accept Christ as Savior, an invitation which he ignored.

We continued with the service. Afterwards, he slipped out before I could speak to him about his desperate condition. I wondered if I would ever see him again. The next night there he sat. That service seemed poured from the same mold as the previous one. Again the Spirit of the Lord pleaded for his repentance. Spiritual tension was mounting. Little did any of us realize that the judgment of God was soon to be poured out upon this man. These were the last efforts of the Holy Spirit to save him from the wrath of God. Again he refused to repent.

What would the third night be like? Would he even come? I was surprised when I arrived at the church to find him there. When it was time to preach, an indescribable heaviness settled over me. Asking everyone to bow their heads and not look about, I extended what I knew to be his last invitation before meeting God's anger. When I met with obstinate refusal, I waited and wept.

He was the only one looking at me, and his cold, defiant gaze filled me with dread. The Spirit of grace began to lift and a sense of God's judgment settled over the church. It was obvious to everyone present that something drastic was about to happen.

In I Corinthians 5:1-5 (NEB), Paul describes in detail a similar instance in the church at Corinth.

I actually hear reports of sexual immorality among you, immorality such as even pagans do not tolerate: the union of a man with his father's wife. And you can still be proud of yourselves! You ought to have gone into mourning; a man who has done such a deed should have been rooted out of your company. For my part, though I am absent in body, I am present in spirit, and my judgment upon the man who did this thing is already given, as if I were indeed present: you all being assembled in the name of our Lord Jesus, and I with you in spirit, with the power of the Lord Jesus over us, this man is to be consigned to Satan for the destruction of the body, so that his spirit may be saved on the Day of the Lord.

That night the Lord directed me to speak words that would radically alter a man's entire future: "Because you have sinned and have consistently refused the grace of God, He now pronounces His judgment upon you. It is certain and irrevocable except you repent. I now turn you over into the hands of Satan for the destruction of your mortal body, that your soul may be saved in the day of judgment. This is done in the hopes that in your sickness you will turn to the Lord in repentance."

The following night his usual seat was vacant—the first time he had missed since the meetings began nearly a week before. Had he simply been insulted at my actions and decided to stay home until the meetings were concluded?

Midafternoon of the next day, the pastor called me. The man's wife (who hadn't attended any of the meetings and was totally unaware of what had transpired) had just called with a message from her husband who was dying. After the service the previous night he had become ill, for no apparent reason, and upon waking the next morning was unable to get out of bed. He was rushed to the hospital. The doctor announced that he was terminally ill with but a few days at most to live. Medical science could not help him.

"But it shall come to pass, if thou wilt not hearken unto the voice of the Lord thy God, to observe to do all His commandments and His statutes which I command thee this day; that all these curses shall come upon thee, and overtake thee . . ." (Deuteronomy 28:15 KJV).

The pastor relayed a request from the man: "If those three young preachers are still at the church, tell them I need prayer, and if God heals me, I'll be out to church. They'll know what I mean."

In his physical distress he had turned to the Lord for the mercy he had scorned when his body was robust and strong. The prayers that he refused in church, he now coveted from his hospital bed. Would he be healed? Indeed *could* he be healed? *Yes!* But he would have to come on God's terms. The curses of Deuteronomy 28 are still potent today, but so is His mercy to all who will call upon Him in truth.

". . . If thou wilt hearken to the voice of the Lord thy God, and wilt do that which is right in His sight, and give ear to His commandments, and keep all His statutes, I will put none of these diseases upon thee, which I have brought upon the Egyptians: for I am the Lord that healeth thee" (Exodus 15:26 KJV).

I interceded on his behalf that afternoon, pleading for God to extend His mercy to him. I felt a deep inner peace

110

born of the Holy Spirit, an assurance that all would be well.

My surprise was evident that night as I walked into church and there sat our friend in perfect health! What had happened? That afternoon after his wife called and requested prayer, the Spirit of God had come into his hospital room and touched his fevered body. The pain left, the fever disappeared, all symptoms of his disease were gone. He felt like a young man again. Remembering his promise, he dismissed himself from the hospital and made his way to the church.

When the invitation was extended for all who would like to commit themselves to Christ and accept Him as Lord, he was the very first to come. The tears of repentance flowed as he determined to turn his back on the extramarital affair in which he had been involved. He was only one of many who were saved and healed in that revival, a visitation of God that began that night.

His sickness had stemmed from sin and a refusal to repent. I know this because the awesome responsibility of pronouncing that judgment fell upon my shoulders. Everyone present in that service heard it publicly.

The Scriptures relate other times when God judged an entire group for one member's sin. Israel, led by Joshua, had entered the land of Canaan. They went from victory to victory, and even the mighty city of Jericho had fallen to the armies of Jehovah. In the seventh chapter of Joshua we read of a surprising defeat at the city of Ai. So small was this city that Joshua decided it was unnecessary to send any more than three thousand soldiers to capture it. Imagine his suprise when thirty-six of his men died in the battle, and the rest of his soldiers ran away, hotly pursued by the men from Ai!

111

Joshua asked the Lord the reason for this defeat. God replied, "Israel hath sinned. . . . Therefore the children of Israel could not stand before their enemies, but turned their backs before their enemies, because they were accursed: neither will I be with you any more, except ye destroy the accursed from among you" (Joshua 7:11a,12 KJV).

An Israelite named Achan had taken a garment and some gold and silver, and had hidden them away in his tent contrary to the direct command of God. He was only *one* man, but God said to Joshua, *"Israel* hath sinned, and *they* have also transgressed my covenant which I commanded *them* . . ." (Joshua 7:11 KJV). Because of one man's sin, the victory was lost and thirty-six men lost their lives.

Disobedience is *serious* business, despite the fact that we often treat it lightly. For this sin of disobedience, God commanded that Achan and his entire family be destroyed. Only then was the power of God able to flow through His people unhindered, causing every alien army to fall before their advance.

How many people are suffering needlessly under the anger of God for sins committed, when with a moment of confession and repentance they could purchase health and strength?

This is by no means the only reason for illness. If it were, this would have been the only chapter in this book. On the other hand, it certainly is not to be glossed over or quickly dismissed. Give it your serious consideration. Allow the Holy Spirit to shine the searchlight of God's love into your heart, illuminating the recesses of your past, to bring to mind any and all unconfessed sins. Then rid yourself of their weight and guilt by thrusting them at the foot of the cross. Confess them before God. Repent of them. Forsake them and find a new strength and vitality throughout your whole being.

Let us also consider an aspect of living related to disobedience which affects the healing process. Have you ever considered how God looks at a complaining spirit? We see some people who can't find anything good in either their church or in other Christians. It is impossible to be in their presence more than a few minutes without feeling the impact of their bitter, complaining spirit.

These people are bad enough in themselves, but left unchecked they infect others. I have known of churches which have been seriously weakened by a complaining spirit. Soon it had infiltrated the ranks of believers to the point that a church split developed.

God takes a dim view of complaining. A time came in the nation of Israel when a hostile, complaining spirit began to predominate. The people murmured not only against God but also against His man, Moses. At this point, God sent fiery serpents into their midst to inflict punishment for their complaining. This punishment continued until they came to Moses and repented for what they had done. Only then did God give the remedy.

When a Christian complains about some brother or sister in Christ, he is doing damage to a part of the body of Christ; and that never escapes God's notice. More often than not, the complaining Christian is, or becomes, a disobedient Christian. If complaint makes its way into the heart, disobedience will not be far behind.

You may say, "But my heart is already full of bitterness and complaining. I'm so disobedient to the Lord. What can I do to rid myself of this plague?"

When Israel arrived thirsty and weary at an oasis in the

desert, only to find that the waters were too bitter for drinking, the people murmured against Moses. Moses cried out to God for the solution and was shown a tree which he was instructed to cut down and cast into the waters. When this was done, the waters became sweet.

The tree typifies the cross of Calvary, where our Lord died so that bitter lives could be made sweet. If your spirit has become embittered through the years, bare your soul in earnest supplication before the cross and apply the power of that tree to the bitter waters of *your* life. Let His sweetness fill your heart until there is no room left for bitterness, complaining and disobedience.

14

Demons and Disease

Have you considered that there may be a link between some sicknesses and demonic power? Many Christians turn their backs on this subject in the hope that it will go away. Still others openly deny that sickness can be caused by demons. Both these groups are poorly informed as to what the Scriptures have to say on this subject. Let us consider a few passages in which demons and sickness are mentioned in the same context.

Later, when Jesus and His party were coming out, they brought to him a dumb man who was possessed by a devil. As soon as the devil had been ejected the dumb man began to talk.

(Matthew 9:32,33 Phillips)

115

Then a devil-possessed man who could neither see nor speak was brought to Jesus. He healed him, so that the dumb man could both speak and see.

(Matthew 12:22,23 Phillips)

. . . And a Canaanite woman from those parts came crying out, "Sir, have pity on me, Son of David; my daughter is tormented by a devil." ". . . Woman, what faith you have! Be it as you wish!" And from that moment her daughter was restored to health.

(Matthew 15:22-28 NEB)

He asked them, "What is this argument about?" A man in the crowd spoke up: "Master, I brought my son to you. He is possessed by a spirit which makes him speechless. Whenever it attacks him, it dashes him to the ground, and he foams at the mouth, grinds his teeth, and goes rigid. I asked your disciples to cast it out, but they failed." Jesus answered: ". . . Bring him to me." So they brought the boy to him; and as soon as the spirit saw Him it threw the boy into convulsions, and he fell to the ground and rolled about foaming at the mouth . . . then Jesus rebuked the unclean spirit. "Deaf and dumb spirit," He said, "I command you, come out of him and never go back!" After crying aloud and racking him fiercely, it came out; and the boy looked like a corpse; in fact many said, "He is dead." But Jesus took his hand and raised him to his feet, and he stood up. (Mark 9:16-27 NEB)

Another time, Jesus was expelling an evil spirit which was preventing a man from speaking, and as soon as the evil spirit left him, the dumb man found his speech, to the amazement of the crowds.

(Luke 11:14 Phillips)

116

In the thirteenth chapter of Luke's Gospel is the story of Jesus encountering a woman in the synagogue who was all bowed over, unable to straighten herself. Although this would appear to be a case of arthritis, Jesus didn't label it so. Calling it a spirit of infirmity, Jesus accused Satan of having bound her for eighteen years. When the Lord rebuked that spirit, the woman was made immediately whole and her back was straightened.

These scriptural instances are proof that many sicknesses are the direct result of demonic activity.

Recently, I had the privilege of praying with a pastor's teen-aged son who had suffered with asthma since he was a young boy. When the demon of asthma was rebuked in the name of Jesus, it threw him to the floor. The powers which had afflicted him for so many years were reluctant to let him go free, but they were powerless before the name of Jesus. Soon he was able to breathe normally again. When I met the young man some months later, he reported that the attacks had not recurred since that day. With joy, we praised the Lord together.

However, not everyone who has asthma is under demonic assault. It is vitally important to distinguish the relationship between sickness and demons. Any sickness (even a common cold) can be caused by demons, but *not every* sickness is caused by them. Cancer is often of demonic origin, but not all cancer is caused by demons.

There is a sense in which all sickness has a *diabolical root*. Sickness is caused by some foreign organism in the body. That organism has a life of its own. The human body, invested with a life-giving spirit, will die if that spirit is taken away.

Likewise, every sickness has a life which allows it to exist and without which it would soon die. All sickness is a

117

form of corruption or death, for illness destroys healthy, living tissue and ultimately, if unchecked, will decimate and exterminate life itself.

Jesus said, "The thief [Satan, or demons] comes only to steal, to kill and to destroy, but I have come to bring them life in its fullness" (John 10:10 Phillips). In this passage, the Lord revealed the mission of Satan: to kill and to destroy. What better way to accomplish this mission than through sickness?

When you become sick, there is an alien life (germ, virus) living in you, a life that God never intended to be there. It lives off *your* strength and saps *your* vitality and health.

We are instructed in the Bible to "pray the prayer of faith" for the sick; but we also have the example (set for us by Jesus Himself) of taking authority over the demons of sickness and rebuking them by the power of the Holy Spirit. There is little sense, or success, in *praying* for a sickness to be healed when the source is demonic in origin. If a river is to stop flowing, the source must be dried up.

It is like a man sitting on a tack and suffering great pain and distress, asking for prayer for relief from the pain. The answer is not to pray for relief, but to stand up and get off the tack. To pray for relief from something of demonic origin temporarily removes the symptoms, rather than destroying the cause.

While conducting services, God will frequently reveal to me the symptoms of someone being healed in the audience or of someone in need of healing. This was the case of a man in Flossmoor, Illinois. As hundreds of people stood at the altar, the Spirit of God revealed to me that one standing there had an affliction which prevented him from lifting his left elbow to shoulder level. Not only was his shoulder affected, but his wrist was almost immovable as well. Not knowing who the man was, I gave a general call for him to identify himself so I could pray with him. I waited. No one responded. I called again for a response. None came.

Then a lady stood up in the audience and volunteered that perhaps it was she, since she suffered with a "tennis elbow." No. The Spirit had directed me to the *altar* area, and had said specifically that it was a *man*.

At this point the enemy began to speak to me: "You know you've made a mistake this time. It's someone in the audience and you said at the altar. Why don't you admit to the people that you've made an error. They'll think highly of you, a man of God who would admit publicly that you had erred."

Then a man standing at the altar spoke up and suggested that perhaps it might be he, as his *right* arm was a little stiff. No again. The symptoms had been given to me exactly—there could be no deviation.

The enemy continued his relentless verbal assault within my mind, suggesting over and over that I had made a mistake. Though not more than five minutes had passed, it seemed like an eternity elapsed until, with tears coursing down his cheeks, a man in obvious turmoil of soul slipped through the crowd. He admitted to the exact physical ailment that the Spirit of God had designated.

Why would a person delay to claim his healing when God longed to make him whole? I wondered.

Through his tears he recounted the years of torment and pain that had begun when he was a child of five. "Something" had happened then, although he couldn't remember exactly what, to disable him. From that time on he was unable to raise his elbow level with his shoulder, nor could he use his wrist with any flexibility. This condition had now persisted for over fifty years with no relief. Although he had sought healing many times, no amount of prayer would change the condition. Why?

The answer was simple: he didn't need to be *healed.* God's Spirit showed me that he needed to be *delivered* from a demonic spirit that had bound him. That same spirit which had held this man for so long knew that the Spirit of God was zeroing in on him, and that his time was limited. As a result, the demon had tried desperately to make me admit to a mistake, which would have allowed him to maintain his grip on that man's body. Since that didn't work, he had attempted to keep the man from coming forward.

As I laid my hands on him and commanded the spirit of infirmity to release him, he fell to the platform, writhing and grimacing. The demon recognized the authority over him through the name of Jesus. In a moment the bondage of over *half a century* was destroyed. Victory had been won, and for the first time since early childhood he had absolute freedom and mobility from his shoulder to his fingertips. I have seen him since his deliverance, and he radiates joy.

Why did this man have to suffer in bondage for over fifty years? Did he never cross paths with someone who could have discerned by the Holy Spirit the source of his dilemma? Probably not. Many theologians deny that there are such things as demons. Others, who admit their existence, deny any connection between them and physical illness. Among those who admit a connection between physical ailments and demonic power, many deny that Christians can be so afflicted.

But the Scriptures deal *specifically* with the Christian's

warfare against such powers. Perhaps the false sense of security—that the enemy cannot touch us at all—is the very means for demonic entrance. We lower our guard, thinking we are invulnerable.

As believers, we do not need to fear sickness or demons, because residing within us is an unearthly power potential. When the Lord left this earth as a human being, He didn't leave us prey to the devil. Consider Matthew 10:1 (Phillips): "Jesus called His twelve disciples to Him and gave them authority to expel evil spirits and heal all kinds of diseases and infirmity."

If anyone argues that this power was given only to the twelve apostles, consider further: "And the *seventy* returned again with joy, saying, 'Lord, even the devils are subject unto us through thy name!' And He said, 'I beheld Satan as lightning fall from heaven. Behold, I give unto you power to tread on serpents and scorpions and over all the power of the enemy: and nothing shall by any means hurt you' " (Luke 10:17-19 KJV).

And beyond the seventy: "These signs will follow those who do believe: they will drive out evil spirits in my name . . ." (Mark 16:17 Phillips).

Let there be no doubt about *every* believer's authority over *all* demonic forces. Settle it in your own mind: Satan has no power sufficient to conquer the believer who knows his rights and who will exercise his privileges in Jesus Christ! You should be victorious, not victimized; the conqueror, never conquered; overcoming rather than being overcome—for "greater is He that is within you, than he that is in the world" (I John 4:4b KJV).

15

Some Surprises

Jesus clearly indicated that "healing is the children's bread" (Matthew 15:26 KJV). It is theirs by divine birthright. Those outside the Kingdom of God have no claim to the promises belonging to the "heirs of God, and joint-heirs with Christ" (Romans 8:17 KJV). The only agreement held out to sinners in God's Word is the promise of redemption. If they will come to Him with repentant hearts He will forgive them and make them His children.

An illustration can be found in Acts 19:13-16:

But there were some itinerant Jewish exorcists who attempted to invoke the name of the Lord Jesus when dealing with those who had evil spirits. They would say, "I command you in the name of Jesus whom Paul preaches." Seven brothers, sons of a chief priest called Sceva, were engaged in this practice on one occasion, when the evil spirit answered, "Jesus I know, and I know about Paul, but who are you?" And the man in whom the evil spirit was living sprang at them and overpowered them all with such violence that they rushed out of that house wounded, with their clothes torn off their backs.

(Phillips)

The men in this story had obviously witnessed the manifestation of God's power at work through the Apostle Paul who was simply obeying Christ's command to cast out devils in His name. Attempting to copy Paul was their undoing, for God's promises of divine protection when dealing with demonic forces were never extended to anyone but believers. As a believer, I can lay claim to every promise in the Word of God and can have the assurance that whatever may happen, He will not fail to perform His Word when it is appropriated in faith.

Having prayed for people around the world, it has been my privilege to witness thousands of miracles. Most who were healed were Christian believers—but certainly not all. And among those unbelievers who were healed, some doubted almost everything, *especially* divine healing. Many of these had actually come to service to poke fun at us.

Now in those same services there were believers who actively attempted to exercise faith for their healing, only to go away disappointed, while the skeptic walked out perfectly well. How is it that the man who has no faith receives that which is withheld from the man who claims to have faith in God's ability to heal?

123

Many people forget that God is sovereign. An old Negro spiritual says, "God is God all by Himself, and He don't need nobody else." There's some good theology in that chorus. God does pretty much what He pleases, anytime He pleases. And whatever He does is perfect—although with our finite minds, we may not be able to discern God's motive. Often the skeptic's healing has been the direct cause of either his salvation or that of someone close to him.

But what about the believers who don't receive healing? Let's face it, some of those whom we call "saints" aren't very saintly. I have known of several people whose lives I've had opportunity to observe closely, and often what I saw caused concern as to the depth of their spiritual experience.

There was a deacon in a church who suffered severely from asthma despite many prayers for his deliverance. How could that sweet gentleman who loved God with all his heart suffer so acutely? Certainly the preacher ought to be able to pray the prayer of faith for such a deserving person.

But an unexpected visit to his farm revealed a different man. Down in the barns he often screamed profanities at his workers, or took the name of the Lord "in vain." Yet, on Sunday he was all sweetness and dedication. Consequently, he never received his healing, and was soon removed from the church board.

The deacon had been such an awful example that his workers became hostile to Christianity. They refused even to listen to the witness of other Christians who also worked for that farmer.

Jesus said, "The slave who knows his master's plan but does not get ready or act upon it will be severely punished. . . ." Reading the truths in previous chapters of this book places the reader in the position of the slave in this passage who "knows his master's plan." To him, therefore, falls the responsibility to rectify those things in his life which have prevented God from healing him.

It becomes obvious that Christians have a great deal more responsibility, due to their knowledge of the Word of God, than a nonbeliever. Their understanding of spiritual things is usually negligible.

Some years ago I ministered in Evangel Temple in Portland, Oregon, with Pastor Joseph Dunets. God manifested His power nightly as many were healed without prayer as they sat in the audience. While I was preaching, my attention was suddenly arrested by the Holy Spirit, who told me that He was doing a miracle of healing on someone in the audience. Immediately I stopped preaching and listened to God's Spirit.

I then said, "God has shown me by the Spirit that He has just healed someone of locked ankle joints in this section to my right. The joints have been in a locked position for some years now, but if you will move them, you will find that God has already healed you."

Instantly, a man rose to his feet sobbing uncontrollably. I called him forward to tell us what had happened. As he came down the aisle, he kept repeating through his tears, "I'm not worthy, I'm not worthy."

When I asked about his condition and what had happened, he related that indeed his ankles had not been flexible for many years. When he had heard me say that God had healed someone of that condition in the section where he was sitting, he experienced a strange sensation and for the first time in many years he had absolute movement of those joints.

But he insisted again and again, "I'm not worthy. I'm not worthy."

"I understand your feeling," I assured him. "None of us is worthy to receive the least of God's favors."

"But you *don't* understand," he went on, "I'm not even saved!"

Within minutes he was repenting of sin and asking Jesus Christ to take over his life. He not only received Christ, but was delivered from alcoholism and addiction to cigarets at the same moment. And it all started with a healing—a healing which, by all rights, he didn't deserve.

Curious, isn't it, how the sovereign Holy Spirit moves to fulfill His purposes? I'm certain that there were Christian people in that same service who went away empty-handed, although they felt as though they had exercised faith for their healings.

Remember what was said in chapter four about the three parts of man: spirit, soul and body. Faith is a function of the spirit. Everything that we receive from the hand of God is appropriated by faith. This is the way He planned it. But faith cannot be *worked up*, neither is it a product of our emotions or our intellect. It is in the spirit that faith is conceived and comes to fruition.

Many people delude themselves into *thinking* they have faith through repetitions of "I believe, I believe, I believe," and all they end up with is a positive mental attitude—which is good in itself, but is not faith.

A Christian may have thought he had achieved faith for healing because of some hot flashes or cold chills. But all he had were hot flashes and cold chills. Our concepts of faith have often been so warped that anything we received from God came in spite of what we called faith, rather than because of it.

126

Faith is a direct product of your spirit taking hold of the promises of God for your need. As the Scriptures have said: "So then faith cometh by hearing, and hearing by the Word of God" (Romans 10:17 KJV).

You would be amazed at how many Christian people do not believe that the entire Word of God is for today. Even some who claim to believe it actually don't. This is borne out not by what they say, but by how they live. Intellectually they have accepted the promises for healing, but in the realm of spirit the intellect will profit nothing.

The Apostle Paul continues this theme in the seventh and eighth chapters of Romans. In chapter seven he describes the painful struggles that raged within him:

> I do not understand my own actions. For I do not do what I want, but I do the very thing I hate. . . . So then it is no longer I that do it, but sin which dwells within me. For I know that nothing good dwells within me, that is, in my flesh. I can will what is right, but I cannot do it. . . . For I delight in the law of God, in my inmost self, but I see in my members another law at war with the law of my mind. . . . So then, I of myself serve the law of God with my mind [soul] but with my flesh I serve the law of sin.
>
> (Romans 7:15-25 RSV)

Chapter eight expands on the subject of flesh-versus-spirit, the topic of much of Paul's works. The apostle clearly indicates that there are various levels of consciousness within man, all of which are to varying degrees striving for the mastery over him. This struggle within man constitutes perhaps the greatest battleground in all the world. This fact is evident in Paul's letter to the church at Galatia (5:16,17): "I mean this: if you are guided by the Spirit you will not fulfill the desires of your lower

127

nature. That nature sets its desires against the Spirit, while the spirit fights against it. They are in conflict with one another, so that what you will to do you cannot do" (NEB).

The soul may be found on either side of evil or good. One day it may serve the spirit and stand for the right, only to bend to the dictates of the flesh the next.

> . . . in us, whose conduct, no longer under the control of our lower nature, is directed by the Spirit. Those who live on the level of our lower nature have their outlook formed by it . . . but those who live on the level of the Spirit have the spiritual outlook. . . . For the outlook of the lower nature is enmity with God; it is not subject to the law of God; indeed it cannot be: those who live on such a level cannot possibly please God. It follows, my friends, that our lower nature has no claim upon us; we are not obliged to live on that level.
>
> (Romans 7:5-8,12 NEB)

The flesh is not able to grasp spiritual truths, yet countless numbers of Christians have never discovered this. In vain they struggle to produce faith through a mental process—*and it simply cannot be done!* They think they have believed, when in reality all they have managed to do is give a mental assent to the promises of God. The spirit has never been given the opportunity to stretch its wings and soar into the heavenlies. They have, by their carnal living or thinking, kept it earthbound. The spirit has been subjected to the will of the flesh instead of the flesh being subservient to the spirit, as God has ordained. So, for these people at least, it is no real mystery why they leave a service without having been healed.

On the other hand, we have a sinner who ventures into a

service where prayer will be offered for the sick. He may have come for any one or a combination of reasons, but he is there and he is listening. Very often what that person hears, he is hearing for the first time. Intellectually it may be an assault upon everything he has ever been taught or believed in.

A person may actually sit in a service and scoff at what he sees, yet later receive a miracle of healing. On the surface that seems incongruous until we realize that a man's outward actions or words are not always a true barometer of what is happening in his spirit. Often a person is the most rebellious just before making a commitment of his life to Christ. Outwardly, and even on a mental level, he may be rejecting Christ, but God is dealing with him by His Holy Spirit on the deepest level of consciousness, within the spirit.

God's transactions, even if they have to do with our physical healing, take place in the realm of the spirit: "Once the Spirit of Him who raised Christ Jesus from the dead lives within you He will, by that same Spirit, bring to your whole being, yes even your mortal bodies, new strength and vitality. For He now lives in you" (Romans 8:11 Phillips).

Some time ago, my wife believed in a faith which did not present Christ as the Savior. Accepting the invitation of some friends, she attended a church that preached the message of salvation and the indwelling of the Holy Spirit.

"I don't believe that!" she grumbled indignantly when the call for salvation was offered. "I'll just sit here and pray one of the prayers we've been taught in our church."

She claimed that the only reason she returned to that church was because she liked the way the minister preached. Mentally, she rejected everything that was preached.

One Sunday evening at the end of the service the pastor extended an invitation to all those who would like to receive Jesus Christ into their hearts for salvation. Donna tells me that her mind was filled with more anger and rebellion that night than ever before.

I'll not go forward and make a fool of myself, she thought. *I'll simply bow my head right here and pray one of my church's prayers.*

As she lowered her head, her heart was seething with anger at the preacher, the message and the church. But then something strange transpired—all her anger and bitterness melted away and she began crying. She wept a prayer of repentance and found Jesus Christ as her personal Savior.

You see, while her reasoning mind was rejecting the message, her spirit was leaping for joy at having finally heard the truth after all those years. The spirit broke through the mind's rejection, and all that she had unconsciously desired to believe became her reality in a moment of time.

On the surface it might seem that God had violated my wife's free will, as though she had no real choice whether to give herself to Christ or not. There she sat, mentally rejecting the message of salvation, yet surrendering her life to Christ at the same moment. Conversely, the desires of the flesh often violate the free will of the spirit.

Each part of man—spirit, soul and body—dominates the will at various times. If we accept what happened to Donna in that light, then there was no diminishing of the freedom of choice. There was rather an ascending of the spirit to its rightful place of dominion.

It is not strange at all that God would work deep within the spirit of a man and he remain unaware of it. But if we are only cognizant of what takes place on a mental or physical level, we will have missed the greatest drama of the ages. The Apostle Paul makes it so clear in I Corinthians 2:9-11:

> But, as it is written: Things which eye saw not, and ear heard not, and which entered not into the heart of man, whatsoever things God prepared for them that love Him. Thus God has, through the spirit, let us share His secret. For nothing is hidden from the spirit, not even the deep wisdom of God. For who could really understand a man's inmost thoughts except the spirit of the man himself?
>
> (Phillips)

Later in this same chapter (verse fourteen) the Apostle elucidates. "But the unspiritual man simply cannot accept the matters which the Spirit deals with—they just don't make sense to him, for, after all, you must be spiritual to see spiritual things" (Phillips).

It is totally conceivable that a sinner may be more tender in his spirit than a Christian who has heard the Gospel all his life. Many Christians develop "hardening of the spirit" by listening to the Word week after week and not obeying it. Paul refers to this kind of Christian in verse fourteen when he uses the term "unspiritual" (the "natural man" in the King James Version). He wasn't speaking there to sinners, but to Christians who were living their lives according to the desires of the flesh. These people cannot comprehend deep spiritual truths, for these are grasped on the level of spirit. They have effectively closed off this avenue of their lives by living as natural men. God will hold them responsible for what they know.

131

Let me state again—faith is not a mental process, neither is it a product of our senses. It is conceived in the spirit of man through a union of his spirit with the Spirit of God. It comes by *no* other means.

According to the Scriptures, a "natural man" is one who is living his life according to the senses rather than obeying the instincts that emanate from his spirit. It is no mystery to me then why people of that nature receive nothing from the hand of God, who has made it expressly clear that "we walk by faith, not by sight" (II Corinthians 5:7 KJV).

"The carnal man sees no further than carnal things. But the spiritual man is concerned with the things of the spirit . . . and this is only to be expected, for the carnal attitude is inevitably opposed to the purpose of God, and neither can nor will follow His law. Men who hold this attitude cannot possibly please God" (Romans 8:5-8 Phillips). Let us then, as Christians who desire to be more like Christ, begin now to cultivate a spirit that is sensitive to the things of God; one that listens to the voice of His Spirit.

We are enjoined repeatedly in the book of Revelation, "He that hath an ear, let him hear what the Spirit saith. . . ." In other words, listen in your spirit for the voice of God. It is so easy in our fast-paced society to fall into the rut of prayerlessness and the habit of simply nibbling at the Word of God.

And when they pray, most Christians have adopted the one-way street approach. That is, they talk to God, but never allow Him to talk to them. As soon as they are through presenting Him with their Christmas list prayer, they get up and leave. Have you ever considered the need to listen after praying?

Suppose you came to talk with me and I gave you my

undivided attention, only to have you turn on your heel and walk away the very moment you were finished speaking, I would be insulted. Perhaps there was something close to my heart that I had wished to share intimately with you, but all you cared about was unburdening your own needs. How often we exhibit this selfish attitude when visiting with our heavenly Father.

In all the furor raised over Transcendental Meditation, the church has overreacted in its attempts to avoid falling into this snare. *Christian* meditation is certainly valid. Isaiah wrote, "But they that wait [meditate] upon the Lord shall renew their strength; they shall mount up with wings as eagles; they shall run, and not be weary; and they shall walk, and not faint" (40:31 KJV).

There is the solution to a powerless prayer life: we must *listen* meditatively for the voice of the Spirit of God to speak to us. When we have finished praying, we must allow ourselves the pleasure of listening as He speaks to us in return. His voice *may* come audibly to your physical ears (I have had that experience only three times in my twenty-some years as a Christian). But more often it will come as a distinct impression, an inner prompting or leading that will later prove to have originated in the mind of God. Frequently, He will simply envelope you in His love until your spirit is drenched with joy.

It is only through use that the spirit of man becomes exercised to instantly recognize the inner movement of the Spirit of God. As we meditate upon Him, we learn to effectively shut out the distractions of the everyday world, and to concentrate our attention on the things of the Spirit. By habitually listening for His voice, you will learn to recognize Him when He speaks. Then you will know how to find God's will for each situation.

Through quiet waiting (meditating) upon God we gain insights into the domain of the Spirit. The flesh becomes relaxed, the mind tranquil. The senses are at rest and in this state we become ready participants in the unfolding drama of the spiritual realm.

Take time for prayerful meditation; it is here that faith is conceived as a vital force. With time and patience you can cultivate this spiritual state until you find yourself walking in the Spirit at all times. Your whole being will be in tune with God's Spirit and faith for your healing will be a consequence of that relationship. Allow your spirit the freedom to dominate both your soul and your body. This is the divine order, and you will be amazed at the changes for good that will transpire. Not only will you find spiritual blessings in abundance but physical well-being also. Your "health shall spring forth as the morning."

16

Can We Live Forever?

People sometimes tell me, "Everyone has to die sometime, but if they kept on getting healed, they would live forever." That reasoning sounds logical, but it isn't scriptural.

The book of Hebrews tells us: ". . . it is appointed unto men once to die. . . ." (Hebrew 9:27 KJV). God has spoken it and, barring the Rapture of the believers first, we will all keep that appointment. No medicine, no surgery, no science can keep us alive indefinitely.

". . . It was through one man that sin entered the world, and through sin death, and thus death pervaded the whole human race, inasmuch as all men have sinned" (Romans 5:12 NEB).

Death entered the world as a consequence of sin. Before the fall of Adam, man was made to live forever in the image of God. Sin resulted in death, accompanied by sickness and disease. But these things were never meant to have a foothold in man—God's crowning creation.

When Jesus said, "the thief comes only to steal, to kill and to destroy, but I have come to bring them life in its fullness" (John 10:10 Phillips), He plainly declared the source of death as the enemy, Satan.

I John 3:8b (RSV) states, ". . . the reason the Son of God appeared was to destroy the works of the devil." Christ didn't do a half-job on Calvary. He paid the full price for all our sins, all our sicknesses and diseases, all our depressions and anxieties; and He paid the full penalty of sin, which was eternal death. If the price has been paid, then there is no need to face the debt incurred by sin. Freedom has been secured through the perfect sacrifice of Calvary.

"Jesus said, 'I am the resurrection and I am life. If a man has faith in Me, even though he die, he shall come to life; and no one who is alive and has faith shall ever die . . .!'" (John 11:25,26 NEB). What a glorious revelation. We need not die eternally, for death is the outworking of sin, which Christ conquered *fully* on the cross.

While "it is appointed unto man once to die," because of Christ's work death does not need to be a grim robbery of a person's life. I do not believe that a saint of God has to die by sickness and disease. The Word of God declares: ". . . Thou takest away their breath, they die, and return to their dust" (Psalm 104:29 KJV). This is the way every saint of God should die. Since the spirit of a man is his life, and the spirit comes from God, then when it is taken back, that man will physically die.

Sickness originated in Satan and sin—certainly not in God. When Christians believe that their sickness is the means God will use to take them home to glory, they imply that God uses Satan's tools in order to accomplish His purpose.

That God would need to use anything of Satan's for any purpose, let alone His child's homecoming, is unreasonable. God doesn't need to work with the enemy to accomplish His divine will. After all, He was the giver of life in the first place. He reclaims that life at His discretion. It was said of the patriarchs that they simply drew their knees up to their chests upon the bed, and went home to God.

A Christian's whole existence—including the way he dies—ought to bring glory to God. A death riddled with disease, pain and agony brings no glory to *Jehovah Raphah,* "the Lord who heals." No saint of God ought to leave this world in physical defeat.

We return again to the question, "If God continues to heal a person of every disease, how would they ever die?"

A very dear friend of mine, a man in his midseventies, was dying of cancer. I was conducting a crusade some distance away when I first learned of his condition. Arriving home, I learned that he had lapsed into a coma; but when he spoke at all, it was to call my name.

When I got to the intensive care unit of the hospital, I was told that he was in a deep coma and could not communicate to anyone, nor could he comprehend. Besides that, doctors were working on him and I would only be in the way. I told them I would wait.

When I was finally allowed into the room it was obvious why the staff didn't want me there. A wasted man lay helpless, with tubes protruding from his body; a man sustained by mechanical devices, covered with sores and bruises. I had come face to face with the work of the enemy. Seeing him, no one would say that *that* is God's way to take one of His children home.

I prayed silently at first and then slipped my finger into my friend's semi-closed fist. Calling him by name, I asked if he knew I was there. His hand closed slightly on my finger. Laying my hands on his body, I prayed that God would heal him of this cancer. It might have been his appointed time to die—but not this way! I asked God to take His child with dignity.

As the prayer ended, he opened his eyes for the first time in days. The coma was over. Shortly, all the tubes were removed, and within a few days he was moved to a convalescent home. There he died peacefully, and not because of cancer.

It is my conviction that when it comes time to go to be with the Lord, He simply sends an angel to call our spirits to Him. I believe that the reason many saints of God do die of some terrible disease is that they have never seen the truth of the Scriptures in this matter, and every promise in the Word of God must be appropriated by faith.

God can, and will, raise men and women from the clutches of a disease-ridden death so that He can take them home with the nobility that ought to accompany such a grand occasion.

"O death, where is thy sting? O grave, where is thy victory?" (I Corinthians 15:55 KJV).

17

A Conclusion to the Matter

"A little later Jesus found him in the temple and said to him, 'Now that you are well again, leave your sinful ways, or you may suffer something worse' " (John 5:14 NEB).

Sin is repugnant to God. It is the antithesis of His nature. Sin in any form cannot remain in one's life without retribution. Judgment follows unconfessed sin as certainly as night follows day.

"Don't be under any illusion: you cannot make a fool of God! A man's harvest in life will depend entirely upon what he sows. If he sows for his own lower nature his harvest will be the decay and death of his own nature..." (Galatians 6:7,8 Phillips).

The judgments of God are sometimes slow in coming to

139

those who have sinned, but they are certain. Don't be misguided into thinking that because someone has seemingly evaded the wrath of God for sins blatantly committed, that judgment isn't following.

Sometimes so much time elapses it is difficult to associate the reaction to the action that precipitated it. For this reason we must submit our lives to the scrutiny of the Holy Spirit and allow Him to search the recesses of our hearts and bring to light any and all unconfessed sin. Unconfessed sin, especially in the life of a believer, wreaks havoc with his well-being, both in spiritual and physical realms. It is futile to think that the prayer of faith can be prayed effectively for someone with unconfessed sin.

In the Scripture at the beginning of this chapter Jesus had healed a lame man at the Pool of Bethesda. Later, upon meeting him in the temple, Jesus warned him not to return to the sinful habits and ways of his past, or he might discover himself worse off than before.

The Lord leaves no room for speculation. If, after you have been healed, you return to the sins of the past (which may have been the original cause of your sickness), it is possible that a greater sickness may befall you.

Are there unconfessed and unforsaken sins weighing upon you? They bring with them the inevitable consequences of which Jesus spoke. The Scriptures are replete with references to sickness coming upon someone as a direct result of sin. Miriam (Moses' sister) was stricken with leprosy for her mockery.

Thousands of Israelites died from the venomous bites of serpents sent among them by God because they had worshipped other gods.

Elisha's servant Gehazi was stricken with leprosy for the sin of covetousness.

Elymas the sorcerer found himself blinded at Paul's command for having attempted to dissuade Sergius Paulus from accepting Christ.

Ananias and his wife Sapphira, both members of the apostolic church, were struck dead for lying to the Holy Spirit. They attempted to keep part of the price of the land they had sold, while pretending to give it all to God.

Sin is no laughing matter in the sight of the Lord! We may treat it lightly—God obviously does not. There may be some who regard the warnings of Jesus as little more than idle prattle. However, disregard for Christ's teachings always brings with it a harvest of sorrow—even though that harvest may be delayed.

We sometimes labor under the misguided delusion that because a sin has gotten old through the passage of time that God writes it off. That is not so. An unconfessed, unforsaken sin of fifty years ago is just as alive today as when the act was originally committed, whether in thought or in deed. The only way to be certain of your spiritual standing with the Lord is by walking in complete fellowship with Him on a daily basis, confessing any and all sins of the past. Forsake them for the newness of life promised in Christ Jesus, and walk after the Spirit—not after the flesh.

It has been my earnest prayer from the time I began this book that it would be a source of healing to all who read it. It is by no means a complete treatise on the subject, but rather an introduction.

There are perhaps as many reasons why some Christians aren't healed as there are Christians in need of healing. Maybe you have read through this book and nothing of what I've written applies to your life. "What do I do now?" you ask.

141

Ask your Father in heaven. Allow the Holy Spirit to probe your mind and spirit, and pray with the Psalmist David, "Search me, O God, and know my heart: try me, and know my thoughts: and see if there be any wicked way in me . . ." (Psalms 139:23,24 KJV).

God is faithful—He will bring to light anything that would hinder you from enjoying all His benefits. Often the probing is unpleasant. It is difficult to look at our failures. But once we have seen our true selves, we must move in whatever direction the Holy Spirit indicates to make the necessary corrections, so that the channel through which healing flows may be clear of all obstructions. You see, it isn't sufficient for us to *know* that something is blocking healing in us; we must also *do* everything within our power to see that our lives are changed in that area.

"And ye shall know the truth, and the truth shall make you free" (John 8:32 KJV). It is only when we live in the light of the truth that we are truly free. The person who is ignorant of the truth gropes in darkness. His is the bondage of wondering why he has not received an answer to his prayer for healing.

Simply allow the Holy Spirit to do His work within your spirit, and you will find Him to be a "life rearranger." He will do in you what you cannot do yourself. Turn all your errors, failures and faults over to Him. Watch Him make something beautiful out of your life. When all is said and done, the heart-searching completed and all obstructions to the flow of His blessings have been removed, then the river of healing will flow over you, and you will be made perfectly whole.

King Solomon once said, "There is no new thing under the sun" (Ecclesiastes 1:9b KJV). This is true. Nothing

I've written in this book is new; all these truths are as old as the Word of God itself. Perhaps the only thing I have done is sort out all these examples and put them together under one cover for easy reference. It is my sincere prayer that this book has ministered to you, the person who has prayed for healing many times, but has received no answer.

As I have preached some of these truths, numerous healings have followed. If, after reading this book and applying its concepts, you have received your healing, please write to me at the address below. State as briefly as possible all the particulars. I will rejoice along with you!

Perhaps you know of some other scripturally valid reason why some Christians are not healed and would like to share this with me for an expanded edition of this book. If so, please share any and all details in your correspondence with me. Especially desired are actual case histories of which you are personally aware.

Thank you, and may God richly bless you!

Reverend Burton W. Seavey
Post Office Box #603
Oak Park, Illinois 60303